A CHRISTIAN'S POCKET GUIDE TO BUDDHISM

Alex G. Smith

CHRISTIAN
FOCUS

Copyright © OMF
www.omf.org.uk

ISBN 1-84550-526-3
ISBN 978-1-84550-526-4

10 9 8 7 6 5 4 3 2 1

Published in 2009
by
Christian Focus Publications,
Geanies House, Fearn,
Ross-shire, IV20 1TW Scotland

www.christianfocus.com

Cover design by Daniel Van Straaten

Printed by Norhaven, Denmark

Contents

Preface

Buddhism and Christianity are two of the great world religions, each with millions of followers across the planet. From their earliest times both have been missionary religions, gaining new followers through outreach and peaceful proclamation of their beliefs. Once enlightened, Buddha immediately proclaimed his message to five Hindu ascetics, who promptly converted, becoming the first Sangha (Buddhist community). Likewise, Jesus Christ called the twelve to follow Him as the first disciples, and gave them the Great Commission (Matt. 28:18-20).

Both religions have suffered through intense persecution and both have survived with great resilience and vitality. Over centuries, while maintaining a solid core of unified fundamental beliefs unique to each, both have developed variegated forms and multiplied different denominations. Both faiths have co-existed for millennia, yet many Christians are largely ignorant of basic Buddhist concepts and many Buddhists know little about Christian beliefs.

This is the age of pluralism, and while the Church continues to reach out, Buddhists are also continuing their mission to the modern world. Buddhist monks conduct missions to tribal groups in Asia, establish missionary training universities, and send missionary monks and laypersons to the West. The freedom of religion in Western nations gives them free rein to propagate Buddhism and receive Western converts, though many Buddhist majority nations do not always grant this freedom to Christian missionaries serving amongst their peoples.

As the twenty-first century unfolds, interaction between Buddhism and Christianity will increase. But while Christians and Buddhists mix freely across the globe, they often do not clearly understand each other. Whether you are travelling on business to Buddhist countries or befriending Buddhists now living in the West and helping them to integrate into society, I hope this book will help you understand your Buddhist friends.

Faith exists in a vast and variegated array of beliefs and denominations, that could never be covered in a book this size. In simplifying complicated concepts, I have left out much more that could be said. I accept full responsibility for any omissions, errors or weaknesses in this text, but hope that I have gone some way towards explaining the basics of Buddhism.

May these observations stir the hearts of Christians and Buddhists to seek with all their being deeper truth, fuller understanding and purer faith.

March 1, 2009
Alex G. Smith, D. Miss
OMF International

One

BUDDHISM TODAY

A Burgeoning Billion

Buddhism began 2,600 years ago in the Indian subcontinent. For centuries it was practised only in Asia, but in recent decades it has experienced considerable growth in the West. Global Buddhism, including folk and popular Buddhism, claims in excess of 1.25 billion adherents, making it the third largest religion in the world. It has become the fastest-growing religion in Australia[1] and there are approximately two thousand Buddhist temples scattered across the USA.

Its dramatic, quiet growth arose through travelling business people, Asian immigrants and refugees, international Buddhist students, US military contacts within Asia, direct missionary efforts and its eclectic absorption of and penetration into other belief structures.

---

1. Johnson and Ryu, *Christian Opportunities in the Changing Demographic Context of Global Buddhism, Sharing Jesus effectively in the Buddhist World*. Lim, Spaulding & De Neui, eds. 2005. Pasadena: William Carey Library

With its emphasis on meditation, morality, ceremonial purity, peace and ethics, Buddhism appears to most Caucasians to be non-threatening. This is in enormous contrast to the common perception of Islam for example. The picture most Westerners have of Buddhism is that of the Dalai Lama – smiling, sophisticated, sweet and serene. As such, Buddhism seems more acceptable and has begun to penetrate and influence many areas of Western culture, even infiltrating the thinking of Christians. For example, one mission leader told of a dream in which he died and thought he had gone to nirvana. He did not say heaven. Pastors occasionally talk of reincarnation as if it is acceptable. In 1982 the US Gallup Poll noted 21 per cent of Protestants and 25 per cent of Catholics believed in reincarnation. Christians sometimes blame their problems on karma. The popular mid-fifties church song, 'A little talk with Jesus makes it right, all right,' included ' Let's keep the prayer wheel turning,' an obvious reference to a Tibetan Buddhist practice.

Historian Arnold Toynbee predicted that the near future would be marked by the 'interpenetration of Buddhism and Christianity,' while sociologist Stephen Warner projects that it will become increasingly difficult to distinguish Christians from Buddhists.

A Syncretistic Mix

The impact of the spread of Buddhism may be illustrated by a kitchen blender. Blend bananas – representing animism[2] or Shintoism[3], apples –

---

2. Animism: the belief that souls or spirits exist in humans, animals, plants and other entities such as natural phenomena and geographic features.
3. Shintoism: a polytheistic and animistic faith, which involves the worship of kami or spirits. Some kami are spiritual beings in a particular place, while others represent major natural phenomenon, for example the kami Amaterasu (the Sun goddess), or the kami Mount Fuji.

depicting indigenous religions like Taoism and Confucianism, and throw in pears – indicative of tribal belief structures, and the composite mixture in the blender still remains a light, creamy colour. Add strawberries though – symbolising Buddhism – and the whole mixture is suddenly saturated with a pink hue. That is precisely the effect of Buddhism. It is eclectically absorbed, dominating but not dislodging these existing beliefs. By this doctrine of assimilation, Buddhism, like a chameleon, changes form from location to location, in whatever ways that make it more acceptable to the local group.

While Westerners and some Buddhist scholars may separate out pure Buddhism from the influence of these other religions, folk Buddhists would see the syncretistic mix merely as facets of the Buddhist religion. Consequently, there is incongruity between orthodox Buddhism and the many varieties of popular Buddhism seen throughout the world today. Scholars list 274 official kinds of Buddhism[4] apart from the diversity of folk Buddhism. A complex spectrum of beliefs make up the Buddhist religion.

Ethical Troubles

This Buddhist spectrum is far from a unified whole and sporadically cracks appear. While these incidents embarrass the Sangha (Buddhist community), to their credit the Buddhist leadership usually confronts aberrant teaching and appropriately deals with breaches and immoral conduct.

---

4. Johnson & Ryu 2005: pp. 32-45

In 1999, a highly respected Thai monk reported that 'aberrant schisms' at a temple in Thailand were 'corrupting the doctrine and discipline of Theravada Buddhism' and 'negating Buddha'. Those who propagated divergent doctrines were promptly disciplined and proscribed. Other charges included 'commercialisation of Buddhism, monks' misconduct and opaque business investments'.[5]

Incidents of priests being defrocked for moral lapses or corruption are not uncommon. Bitter rivalries exist among some of the sects or divisions of Buddhist followers. In Japan, the expensive and ornate Shohondo, the grand worship hall at the foot of sacred Mt. Fuji, was destroyed under orders of the high priest, after prolonged internal conflicts and power struggles among the thirty sects worshipping there. The Aum Shinrikyo (Supreme Truth) was a Buddhist cult in Japan. Their misinterpretation of Buddhist thought led to a lethal attack on the Tokyo subway system in 1998.[6]

Buddhism has divisions and deviant groups, just like all religions, but despite these, Buddhism is expanding.

Resurgence and Resistance

The First International Buddhist Propagation Conference was held in Kyoto, Japan in 1998; a key discussion centred on the growing concern to protect existing Buddhist populations from religious change. Prominent Buddhist leaders from seventeen Asian countries attended and

5.   Source Bangkok Post Feb 19, 1999
6.   Source Newsweek June 1, 1998

Dr K. Sri Dhammananda, a leading Buddhist scholar and prolific author, claimed; 'Poverty and ignorance were exploited to convert innocent Buddhists and to disrupt their ancient cultures and practices. Many countries which were Buddhist are in danger of losing their Buddhist predominance due to these despicable methods employed by so called "evangelists".'

In most South-East Asian countries some restrictions on spreading the gospel are already legally in place, although not always enforced. However, in Laos pressure has been put on Christians to attend anti-religion seminars propagating the government's party line. Officials demand each person sign documents before the authorities, affirming that they will resign from all foreign religions, involvement in which is interpreted as being illegal activity. Their signatures give officials the right to punish them appropriately for any infractions. A similar movement is afoot in Vietnam, particularly targeting ethnic-minority Christians. Some radical Buddhists in Myanmar have declared Christian radio broadcasting a threat to Buddhism, and have specifically named certain Christian agencies as culpable. Extremists have distributed documents listing systematic methods for eliminating Christianity.[7]

On the other hand, aggressive Buddhist outreach is increasing. In 2000, *Civilisation* magazine declared a 'Buddha boom' was escalating in the West. It is claimed that a Buddhist temple in California, one of the largest in the USA, was built primarily as a Buddhist missionary training centre to reach Westerners.

---

7.   Maranatha Christian Journal, Oct 1, 1999

Buddhist universities are also becoming more prolific. For example, Soka Gakkai International (SGI), a relatively new Buddhist movement, constructed the new Soka Buddhist University in California. Twelve of the seventeen administrators are SGI members.[8] In early 2000, an area in Hollywood home to about 70,000 Buddhist Thai was dedicated 'Thai Town' by some Buddhist monks. In Northern Thailand Buddhist monks' outreach into tribal villages resulted in whole villages of Karen and other tribes becoming Buddhist, including some former Christian villages. Furthermore, on one day in 2000, two hundred tribal men from northern Thailand were ordained as monks at one Buddhist temple ceremony in Bangkok.

Buddhism Adapting Locally

With the Dalai Lama's example and encouragement, Buddhism has been made more palatable to North Americans and Europeans. Tibetan Buddhists have endeavoured to reduce the magic and tantric elements, and Buddhist rituals have been advertised as 'cultural events.' Sand mandalas, for example, have been set up in many cities in the West and promoted as visitor attractions, resulting in wide attendance. But these mandalas are spiritually symbolic constructions meant to invoke the spirits and deities to be present and resident. They are ritually destroyed as a Buddhist representation of the impermanence and emptiness of life.

---

8.   Los Angeles Times, dated October 2, 1999

The Dalai Lama's 1996 book on Jesus attracted some Christians to Buddhism. His popular writings have appealed to others through their emphasis on 'ethics for the new millennium', claiming to hold the key to happiness, liberation, tolerance and 'peace without religion'. Recently, the Dalai Lama's speeches added forgiveness to the promises of Buddhism, though forgiveness cannot be found within the Buddhist system of karma and self-deliverance.

Fundamental Buddhism relegates women to an inferior position. In Theravada Buddhism, until a woman is reborn as a man she has no hope of attaining nirvana, but doctrines like this are rarely taught in the West.

This low-key approach has influenced many Westerners. Numerous Hollywood films have promoted Buddhist tenets and philosophies. Some popular actors, television stars and even several prominent politicians openly identify themselves with Buddhism and well-known business people and economic firms have taken on 'Boardroom Buddhism' to manage stress.

Buddhist missions have adopted church evangelistic methods and strategies. For example, in Korea traditional Buddhist temples were isolated up in the mountains away from population concentrations. Today, however, Korean monks have moved down into urban centres to set up 'house temples'. For decades Soka Gakkai has used the 'cell group' approach, like many churches do. To be more customary to those living in traditionally Christianised Western cultures, Buddhists have adapted Christian forms of singing and music in their services, have begun to preach in the vernacular language, and have added Sunday schools to their programmes. Some church buildings have also been converted into Buddhist temples. In Myanmar Buddhist monks have begun to use the Bible selectively to preach and interpret their doctrines, as a way of bringing in and converting Christians.

Buddhism is on the move.

TWO

UNDERSTANDING BUDDHISM

How Did Buddhism Start?

Gautama Siddhartha was a Hindu prince, born in a palace of the Shakya tribe in northern India (now Nepal), about the time of the biblical prophet Daniel. In the sixth century before Christ, Gautama became the historically recorded Buddha and expounded the Buddhist teachings he received through enlightenment. His life is divided into three main phases:

Three periods

First was affluence. Gautama's father pampered him with luxury and pleasure, protecting him from seeing pain and suffering, and preventing him from contact with death and decay. By nineteen, he was married to his cousin, Yasodhara, and at twenty-nine had a son, named Rahula (meaning chain or fetter).

The second period started when, one day Gautama went beyond the protective walls of the palace and saw four people – an old man, a sick person, a dead body and an ascetic. This shocked Gautama, and that night, without waking his wife or young son, he left the palace. Buddhists call this The Great Renunciation. For the next six years, he followed the rigorous austerity of an ascetic, disciplined life. One day, because of weakness from fasting, he almost drowned while bathing and realized that this stringent path did not provide the answers.

He returned to the city of Bodh Gaya where he started on the third period; seeking and inquiring. He deeply meditated under the Bodhi fig tree for seven weeks and during this time received enlightenment, including the Four Noble Truths:

1) All is suffering
2) The cause of suffering is desire and craving
3) The solution is to extinguish desire and craving
4) The method is through the Eightfold Path.

The Buddha, as he was now called, rejected the existence of Creator God and the soul, and saw other gods or spiritual beings as inconsequential, for they also were caught in the cycle of life. He taught that karma (cause and effect) of past lives resulted in the constant circle of birth, death, and rebirth. He believed the only way to be free of this is through your own efforts. The teachings of the Buddha that lead to enlightenment are known as Dharma. Immediately he found five ascetic men and preached to them in Deer Park. They were converted and formed the first Buddhist sangha or community. He also saw many family members and famous people become his followers. The Buddha died about 480 B.C., probably of food poisoning.

Expansion

For the next 200 years Buddhism was confined to north India. Then it expanded dramatically under

King Asoka (274–232 B.C.). He consolidated his conquests by sending out Buddhist missionaries to preach and convert the people. Thus, all of India came under Buddhist sway. Asoka also sent his son, Mahendra, as a missionary to Ceylon (modern-day Sri Lanka) where he converted the king. Buddhism spread into China, Afghanistan and as far away as Greece and Cyrene (North Africa). Later it expanded through Korea, Japan, Indonesia, Mongolia and most of South-East Asia. Within 1,500 years, Buddhism became a major influence over all aspects of Asian culture, and has remained so ever since.

Assimilation

Wherever Buddhism spread, it had a vacuum cleaner effect, sucking up indigenous religions under its broad umbrella. It dominated and integrated local belief structures, but did not dislodge nor destroy them, and so was readily accepted.

Buddhism has also produced a strong national and racial identity and this has become the strongest obstacle to evangelism and barrier to conversion. 'To be Thai, Burmese, Tibetan, Lao ... is to be Buddhist.' The strength of this identification among Asian peoples was seen when the stringent pressure of communism was removed in the 1990s. Though Buddhism was repressed, restricted and taught against for years in places like Mongolia, Vietnam and China, it immediately returned to its original influence, as soon as the restrictions were removed. It was simply ingrained in the national identity. There is some evidence this is beginning to change but it is still a significant obstacle.

Major Schools and Cults

While 'ideal' beliefs are common in many religions, the 'real' beliefs and behaviour of followers is often quite different. Many follow basic Buddhist precepts, but the majority also practice many of the elements the Buddha saw as questionable, including worshipping him and belief in gods, spirits, ghosts and many other indigenous forms of religion. Thus a multitude of different types of Buddhism have proliferated. Truly there is little pure Buddhism on earth, except among some dedicated intellectual Buddhists and long-term committed monks.

The plethora of Buddhist 'denominations' with their innumerable cults is quite astounding. Here Buddhism certainly shows its tolerance, without sacrificing its basic integrative doctrinal foundations. Japan alone has more than 170 Buddhist cults. In 1999, China's PRC authorities outlawed the Falun Gong cult, which incorporates T'ai Chi with Buddhist meditation and practices, claiming over 160 million adherents. Currently Falun Gong is administered and run out of New York via the Internet. Another major Buddhist sect emphasises Avolokiteshvara, a female-looking bodhisattva of compassion, originally from India. The sect has revived and expanded worldwide, particularly during the late 1900s. It is known as Kannon in Japan; Chenrezig in Tibet and Kwan Yin among Chinese. Tibetans believe the Dalai Lama is a reincarnation of Avolokiteshvara.

However, there are primarily two major schools of Buddhism:

1. Theravada

This is a conservative school of Buddhism, also known as Southern Buddhism, and tends to be found mainly in Sri Lanka and South-East Asia. It accounts for about 250 million people.

2. Mahayana

This is a more liberal school, also known as Northern and Eastern Buddhism. It covers the globe, but has major concentrations in East Asia. It accounts for approximately 1,200 million folk Buddhists. Major branches of the Mahayana school include Tendai, Zen, Pure Land, Nichiren, Soka Gakkai, Tibetan and so forth.

Some modern scholars consider a third school to be Tibetan, also called Lamaism, Tantrism, Vajrayana, or Mantrayana. Globally, the Tibetan form is the smallest group with under 20 million followers. Though it has three major lamas from three separate lineages, many Tibetan Buddhists acknowledge the Dalai Lama, leader of the Geluk lineage, as its visible head. It has become quite popular in the West, because of the presence, policies and political cause of the Dalai Lama.

Buddhism is the integrating and identifying religion of over one billion people.[1] In Thailand ninety-five per

---

1.   Johnson and Ryu, 2005

cent claim to be Buddhists, mostly of the Theravada school. Approximately seventy per cent of the Japanese adhere to some form of Mahayana Buddhism. Millions of Westerners, often unofficially, practice some kind of popular Buddhism – Buddhist scholars call them lounge-chair or hyphenated Buddhists, characteristic of the increasing interpenetration of Buddhism and other religions.

Basic Buddhist Beliefs

As we have already said, Buddhism exists in a plethora of forms, but the following fundamental beliefs are universal amongst all Buddhist groups.

Meditating on the Middle Way (avoiding dualistic extremes), the Buddha, Gautama Siddhartha, intuitively realized the Four Noble Truths which explained the condition, cause and cure of universal suffering. The Buddha taught that by following the Eightfold Path of self-effort one could escape life's suffering. This Eightfold Path would help you to attain enlightenment by eliminating all desires and cravings (the cause of suffering), and so allow you to enter nirvana, a state of escape; a breaking free from the endless cycles of birth and rebirth.

This idea of karma and rebirth is borrowed or adapted from Hinduism, out of which Buddhism developed. From the start the Buddha rejected or ignored the existence of all gods and spiritual beings, including the concept of humans as living souls. He considered everything to be changing, illusionary and impermanent. Only by self-deliverance and doing good can one hope to proceed to a better reincarnation and eventually, after tens of thousands of births and rebirths, hopefully attain nirvana.

The Four Noble Truths

The Four Noble Truths were the initial teaching of the Buddha when he was first enlightened. As such they are considered the essence of Buddhism.

Truth 1: Life is suffering because all is impermanent, imperfect and unsatisfactory.

Truth 2: Suffering is caused by desiring or craving attachment to all forms of illusion or impermanence and emptiness.

Truth 3: To escape suffering one must stop these cravings and eliminate desires.

Truth 4: The way to end suffering and be freed from desire is to follow the Noble Eightfold Path.

The Noble Eightfold Path

The Noble Eightfold Path is the way to end suffering and attain nirvana. The eight principles, accomplished by your own effort, are divided into three groups:

Wisdom

This wisdom cultivates truth from one's experiences and purifies the mind so it can develop spiritual insight about the true nature of things. It is made up of:

1. Right View: understanding the world as it really is and not just as it appears.

2. Right Intention: resolving to rid oneself of wrong or immoral conduct and to commit oneself more fully to the spiritual path.

Ethical Conduct

The discipline of restraining one's body from un-wholesome acts, so that one's mind can focus on the spiritual path. It involves:

3. Right Speech: Avoiding things such as lying, slandering, divisive talk, abuse and gossip.

4. Right Action: acting in helpful ways that do not bring harm to oneself or others such as not killing, stealing, getting drunk, or acting irresponsibly, particularly in sexual matters.

5. Right Livelihood: engaging in occupations that do not harm oneself or others, but assist all to live honourable, healthy lives.

Concentration

The mental discipline to control one's thoughts, using techniques such as meditation.

6. Right Effort: the persistent effort to rid oneself of all harmful thoughts and actions and to practice the Dharma appropriately.

7. Right Mindfulness: keeping your mind alert, so all actions are deliberate and considered, aware of what one is doing, thinking and feeling.

8. Right Concentration: stilling the mind to attain to full concentration until meditative absorption of peaceful inner calm is reached.

Sila (Moral Code)

The Sila or Five Precepts are the basic principles of Buddhist ethics. They are not laws as such, but suggested moral attitudes or training rules that will help followers lead a more devoted life and progress towards enlightenment. The Five Precepts are as follows:

1. Do not take life. Avoid causing harm to other beings.

    This refers to killing people, animals and living things, and is the basis for some Buddhists following a vegetarian lifestyle. Some extend the precept to include plants and insects.

2. Do not take what is not given. Avoid exploiting or manipulating others

    More than just do not steal, this is sometimes expanded to include taking anything unless someone explicitly gives it to you.

3. Do not distort facts. Avoid untruthfulness.

    Though often interpreted as 'do not lie' this has a wider intention, avoiding gossip, boasting, frivolity or negativity, including exaggeration or even simply phrasing that could be misinterpreted by the hearer.

4. Do not misuse the senses. Avoid abusive, obsessive or manipulative sex.

    Buddhists list six senses; touch, hearing, sight, smell, taste and thought. Overindulging any of these, for example, having sex too frequently, listening to music too often, seeking out beauty in your surroundings, eating rich foods or spending too much time in thought at the expense of action are considered misuse.

5. Do not use self-intoxicants. Avoid clouding the mind with drugs.

    Self-intoxicants are any substance that changes your mental state, whether drugs, alcohol, Prozac, coffee or even chocolate!

Some schools of Buddhism extend these to eight or even ten precepts. As these are only suggested rules for training, they can be interpreted by the follower and kept to varying degrees, as the individual sees fit. Some Buddhists will drink coffee but not eat meat, while others will live unmarried with their partners, but not drink alcohol. Even those who do not keep any of the Sila, will still hold them as their moral foundation, and the rules that govern society.

The Cycle of Samsara

All beings crave pleasure and desire to avoid pain. Being controlled by these drives they continue to experience a cycle of birth, death and rebirth known as Samsara. This generates suffering (*dukkha*). The aim of Buddhism is to escape from or end this repeated cycle of life by freeing oneself from desire which causes suffering.

Karma: Cause and Effect

Karma drives the cycle of life, death and rebirth, which causes suffering (*dukkha*) for each being. Everything a person does has good or bad intention behind it. This intention, as well as the action itself, determines the effect. The karmic effects of cumulative actions and thoughts produce suffering.

To overcome this suffering a person must follow the Noble Eightfold Path.

Rebirth and Stages of Being (Bhumis)

The Buddhist belief is that when you die, you begin life again. This is repeated many times over. Mahayana Buddhists claim a person can be reborn into any of six major realms of existence, while the Theravada School acknowledges only five, excluding the realm of the bodhisattvas. Both schools usually combine the hells and demon realms together.

Older teaching explains these six realms are comprised of thirty-one separate levels or planes of existence (*bhumi*).[2] The amount of one's good or bad karma determines the plane into which rebirth occurs.

The four lowest planes are realms of deprivation, known as Worlds of Misery (*apayas*). These are:

- Demons, also known as *Asura* or *Titans*, are beings consumed by anger.
- Ghosts or unhappy spirits, known as *Peta* or *Preta*, are beings devoid of happiness.
- Animals dwell in the animal realm, known as *Tiracchana*. It is characterized by suffering, fear and violence.
- Hells – there are eight major hells, collectively known as *Niraya* or *Naraka*. Each hell has a different form of suffering. These are thought to exist below the earth's surface.

---

2. Source: The 31 Planes of Existence, Suvanno Mahathera, Buddha Dharma Education Association Inc, Inward Path, Penang Malaysia. 2001.

Directly above these four realms is the human being realm. Then above that are six stages of the demi-gods (god-like spiritual beings including the bodhisattvas). These seven Sensuous Worlds are full of happiness, but this happiness is connected with desires. The seven worlds are:

- Six *Kama-Loka* are the realms of the demi-gods and bodhisattvas. These are full of greater pleasures than those experienced on earth, but the demi-gods desire to be born back into the human realm where they can make merit and attain the enlightenment.
- The human realm, known as *Manussa-Loka*, is a mixture of suffering and bliss.

Higher than these eleven lower planes are another twenty *Brahma* or *deva* (gods) realms. These twenty planes are akin to kinds of sensual temporal heavens (*jhanic bliss*). The Buddha saw these deva as part of the oneness of nature. Consequently these gods are non-eternal beings who still experience karma and rebirth too. The twenty Brahma worlds include:

- Four *Loka* or realms are inhabited by *Arupa*, a type of Brahma that is formless and immaterial.
- Sixteen *Loka* are occupied by the *Rupa* – devas of form and material.

The thirty-one bhumi constitute *Samsara* and are all part of the *dukkha* – the truth of suffering. The only way to escape these realms is by enlightenment.

Heavens and Hells

Buddhism has many levels of heavens and of hells, but these are not the same as the Christian heaven or hell. Nor are the Buddhist heavens the same as their nirvana, which is more of a permanent state, somewhat like the Christian concept of heaven. All heavens and hells in the Buddha's view are temporary states, where the occupants are dealing with cravings and desires as well as working out the consequences of karma. The gods (*devas*) revel in pleasures in various heavens only to be reincarnated usually in one of the hells. The highest twenty Brahmas' realms are inhabited entirely by males. However, only from the human realm can one become enlightened.

Impermanence

Known in Buddhism as *anicca*, the doctrine of impermanence or transitoriness is the belief that all things and experiences are changeable and impermanent. Everything is in constant flux and nothing lasts. As a result, attachment to or desire for any of these illusionary things is futile and only leads to suffering.

Concept of No Self

Known in Buddhism as *anatta*, the doctrine of soullessness or absence of self. Buddhists believe that everything is impermanent, including the human soul. Instead of each person having a permanent essence, what Christians call a soul or spirit, that remains constant and existent through death and rebirth, Buddhists believe there is no underlying, persistent reality of self, ego, soul or spirit.

Nirvana

Nirvana is the goal of Buddhism. It is the state of enlightenment, when all craving and desire cease and the knowledge of true reality, as Buddhists see it, is attained. An individual reaching enlightenment is finally released from Samsara, the cycle of life and suffering. The Mahayana School believes that, since each sentient being already has the Buddha nature as a principle, meaning each is capable of being enlightened, at enlightenment then each becomes a Buddha. Interestingly, only from the human realm can any being, including gods (*devas*), reach enlightenment and attain nirvana.

Worldview

The mental map of the Buddhist mindset or worldview is like one single circle representing the whole. Everything that exists is within that circle. No being exists independently on its own, either in, of or by itself. Everything is bound inextricably together. This interdependence is an important Buddhist doctrine that binds all individuals to the wheel of life through sequences of karmic cause and effect. This monistic view of the world is a basic assumption of Buddhism. It affects the way they think and what they believe about the world around them. This influences their penchant for ecology also. Comprehending their worldview is essential to understanding Buddhists. The worldview of Buddhists rejects a Creator God who is outside of and apart from creation, which is the view that Christians, Muslims and Jews hold. This alternative is best illustrated by two circles, a large one representing the creation with a smaller one above and outside of it, representing Creator God. Thus this system is dualistic. The Creator initiates, sustains and superintends His creation. While being separate from it, Creator God is intimately concerned for creation and is personally involved for its good.

Three

BUDDHIST PRACTICES

Morality, merit and meditation comprise the central practices of Buddhism.

The Middle Way

This is the practice of non-extremism; a way of balanced living based on moderation and avoiding dualistic extremes. It is said that Buddha practised this before he was enlightened. This avoidance of extremes was recently shown in the peaceful protests in Myanmar when many Buddhist monks actively joined and marched together with the protestors. The monks took a middle path between passively accepting the intolerable conditions on one hand and reacting forcibly with anger and rebellion on the other.

Is Buddhism Always Peaceful?

A misconception is that Buddhists are always peaceful so they never react violently. Today's Buddhism is socially active and some followers often use violent means in protesting against unfair practices. In Burma there are regular violent clashes between Buddhists and Muslim people. Some Buddhist countries persecute Christians too. Sri Lanka, Tibet and South-East Asia have displayed uncharacteristic violence against authorities and churches in recent decades. Not all Buddhists act so violently but, like Christians, Muslims, Hindus and Jews, Buddhists are not always peaceful and serene. Murder, rape, theft and corruption are commonly experienced within Buddhist communities too.

Meditation

Meditation has two primary forms; tranquillity (*samatha*) and insight (*vipassana*). The use of particular postures (mudras) and mantras (powerful syllables or words) helps focus concentration. Other techniques include visualization, flashes of insight and yoga, with its 1,013 mantras, each dedicated to a different deity.

Some key differences between Buddhist and biblical meditation are:

Buddhism	Christianity
Disengaging the mind and letting it go blank	Engaging the mind with God's Word, deliberately considering Scripture
Suppressing the rational processes to achieve mental calm	Utilising rational processes, bringing every thought captive to the obedience of Christ (2 Cor. 10:5)
Becoming detached with an empty, neutral mind to gain personal inner quietness	Focusing the mind and heart on God, not self, connecting wtih God in the Spirit
Concentrating on one central narrow point and attaining self-insight	Concentrating on listening to God, His Spirit and His Word
Self-focusing and non-relational becoming one with the Buddha nature or a Buddha world	Relating to God's person, character, attributes, works, grace and mercy. Active in praising and thanking Creator God.

Rites, Rituals and Festivals

The most important rite that Buddhist monks
conduct is funerals. The proper death rites
are crucial. In Theravada Buddhism until the
corpse is properly cremated it cannot continue
on into the next rebirth. However, in Mahayana
Buddhism   burial   is   common,   following
appropriate rites. Another important Buddhist
rite is that of entry into monkhood, whether for
a brief period or for life. Some of the festivals
also relate directly to monks such as *Kathina*,
around October, when robes and offerings are
made for the monks. A set of sacred festivals
are held in conjunction with the Buddha's
birth (*Vesakha*), his first sermon (*Asalha*), his
return from heaven after teaching his mother
(*Assayuja*), and the sending out of the first
Buddhist missionaries (*Kattika*). New Year
festivals are commemorated at different times
for different nations. It is usually about April
for Theravadas. In eastern Mahayana a group of
festivals revolve around the birth, enlightenment
and death of the Bodhisattva *Kuan Yin*, not the
Buddha. Some festivals in Mahayana centre
about cultural issues like ancestor festivals
such as Hungry Ghost for Chinese or *O-bon* for
Japanese. The lunar calendar determines the
dates of all Buddhist festivals, including the
weekly Buddha Day, similar to the Sabbath,
when the faithful visit temples and listen to
monks preaching the *Dharma*.

Symbols and Aids

Buddhism has a multitude of symbols, many borrowed
or adapted from Hinduism. For example, the *chakra*
(a wheel with spokes) symbolizes the cycle of life or
the wheel of *Dharma*. The lotus (water lily) features
prominently in postures and offerings. The Bodhi tree
also plays a prominent role. The *Naga* (*Mucilinda*),
the mythical multi-headed serpent, protects Buddha's
head from the elements; his coiled body is Buddha's
throne. In Mahayana the dragon is often used in place
of the *Naga*. The swastika is common in Buddhism
as an auspicious sign with many meanings, such as
the *Dharma*, universal harmony, balance of opposites,
resignation, longevity, prosperity and peace. Swastikas
are often found on the chests, palms, soles of feet and
foreheads of images of the Buddha and on temples.
Prayer beads (rosaries), prayer flags and prayer *Mani*
stones abound. Power-infused sounds, syllables,
phrases and drawings are utilized symbolically such
as in chanted *mantras*, magical *tantras* and pictorial
yantras. Sacred cloths and threads, holy water,
relics and various images are employed in rites and
ceremonies. *Tangka* pictorial scrolls and *Mandala*
diagrams of Buddha worlds become the focus for
meditation. *Mudras* (postures) and yoga poses
symbolically represent dedication to various deities.

Buddhist Attitudes

In many respects Buddhists have aspirations,
ambitions and desires for education, wealth and
advancement like most people on earth.

Wealth

In Buddhist societies being rich or powerful is believed to be an evidence of good karma from a previous life, while extreme poverty results from bad karma. This is not conditioned on the current morality of the life one lives. However, pursuit of wealth, career or status, and all they entail – hedonism, materialism, appearance and so on – does not fit with the guidelines of the Eightfold Path, so may be viewed as unadvisable by some more devout Buddhists.

Health

Those afflicted with illness or disabilities view these in the same way they view poverty – a result of their bad karma. This can lead to exclusion from society and many forms of prejudice or discrimination, with the attitude that the illness was self-inflicted and in that respect deserved.

Environment

Green ecology, with its concerns for the environment, and vegetarianism, with its focus on preserving all forms of life, fit well into the Buddhist framework. Aldous Huxley, in his book *Island* (1962), declared, 'Elementary ecology leads straight to elementary Buddhism.' Christians also have a mandate from God to care for life, the earth and its resources (Gen. 1:27-30; 2:7-8, 15).

Politics, Peace and Social Order

The Middle Way instils an avoidance of extremes in Buddhist culture. As such, peace and harmony are of key importance. Justice, corruption, social care and so on, are as important to Buddhists as they would be to anyone, but the way Buddhists ideally react to these issues would be through peaceful protest and proclamation of the Noble Truths. The Sila and Eightfold Path clearly give Buddhists a moral stance against crime, violence, social injustice and drug culture for example. As discussed earlier though, the extent to which these beliefs are practised, and in what form varies.

In some of the areas above, the Buddhists and Christians converge and these can be the basis for building bridges together for the good of society and the planet, especially in a time when the mixing or interaction between these religions is increasing.

Four

BUILDING RELATIONSHIPS

In 1974 the bulk of non-Christian populations were concentrated in Asia[1], primarily Muslims, Hindus, Chinese and Buddhists.[2] Thirty years later the statistics have not changed much.[3] Even Mao Zedong's three decades in control of China, denouncing religion and promoting communism, did not destroy the influence of Buddhism. Certainly changes occurred, but Buddhist thinking, mixed with animistic beliefs, still pervades much of the Asian worldview today. Buddhists are among the largest group of unreached peoples. China alone has a population of 1.3 billion – a fifth of the world's population and about a quarter of the four billion unevangelised today. Since 2000, many urban professionals and intelligentsia in China's cities have adopted Buddhism seriously. The majority of Buddhists we meet are likely to be from an Asian background.

Irrespective of religion, Western and Eastern cultures have significant differences. Looking at

---

1. Lausanne statistics, given in Ralph Winter's plenary paper at Lausanne, July 1974.
2. Winter, Ralph D. 'Who are the Three Billion?' *Church Growth Bulletin*, Vol. XIII, No. 5, May, 1977: pp. 123-126
3. Johnson and Ryu 'The Changing Demographic Context of Global Buddhism,' 2005

modern-day Asians commonly dressed in Western attire, it's easy to think they are just the same as our Caucasian friends down the street, except that they speak different languages. However, their cultural values and mindset may be as different to Westerners as chalk is to cheese. Buddhism has deeply influenced Eastern culture, even if the individual does not identify themselves as a Buddhist, in the same way that Christianity has historically influenced Western culture. When interacting with Buddhists, especially those from Asia, we need to be sensitive to the nuances of their cultural backgrounds. Here are some general differences which need careful handling.

Gestures

What a person finds welcoming or offensive will be largely dependent on their culture. A Western Buddhist would respond very differently to an Asian Buddhist. Here are some general pointers on interacting with Buddhist peoples, particularly those from Asian backgrounds.

Some actions or gestures of Westerners are offensive to Asian people, such as yelling, speaking loudly or pointing at someone. Beckoning with fingers or the hand with palms turned up is offensive; palms need to be down. Sitting on a table or desk or sitting with crossed legs is seen as impolite or disrespectful, as is giving someone something by throwing it to them or sliding it across the table. Touching someone's head or reaching above it is unacceptable behaviour as the head is considered high and a sacred part of humans. Snapping fingers at someone, slapping a person on the back, looking directly into their eyes – especially of women – or using the foot to point to something are inappropriate. Showing affection in public, especially kissing or touching the opposite sex, should be avoided. Asians also are generally conservative in dress or clothing and also modest, not exposing their bodies. Westerners need to be careful not to overtly breach these norms. While eating meat is not a big issue, killing an insect in front of them may be. Such things may be accepted among Westerners, but should be avoided before Buddhists or Asian peoples.

Remember though to treat people as individuals. Even within these Asian contexts, urban young people for example may have much more modern and often Western attitudes than previous generations. Be sensitive as you get to know someone and find out how best to communicate.

Activities

Most healthy, happy and upright activity is beneficial in developing relationships. Asians love to have fun and enjoy games and sports as well as walking and talking together. Mostly they will spend time in same-gender groups, and often they will hold hands and be openly affectionate. This does not necessarily mean they are gay. On the other hand more care needs to be exercised in male/female paired relationships. Innocent though these may seem, misunderstanding of expectations and obligations may arise from their perspective. It is often better and more appropriate to organise group activities built around informal friendships than to engage in isolated pairing off of boy-girl. Watching films or sports on television, or playing games in groups are acceptable means of interacting socially. Personal communication and contact is important. Phoning and arranging times to visit them may be more effective than e-mailing. Texting is common. Asians love to eat; meals are fun times and relational opportunities too, whether done in homes or in restaurants. For some, raucous humour, observing nudity or heavily consuming alcohol might be embarrassing, and not conducive to cementing relationships. Offering help is encouraged, but care needs to be exercised in gift giving, as some, such as Japanese, likely will feel obligated to give back an even better gift. Wisdom and moderation are required.

Family

Asian psychology has significant variations to our Western make-up. Their families play stronger roles in decisions. An individual's identity is linked to the family, more than the individual is in the West. Asian families tend to criticise the individual member, rather than listen to and help them with their problems. Efforts focus on conforming them to the family norms more than assisting them to solve their issues. Consequently, youth and adults tend to share their problems with close friends more than with relatives.

Asian societies are not as open as Western ones, but are more reserved and demure. They do not readily say 'Hi' to everyone as the Western habit frequently is. Asians feel they have limited choices, often due to family and cultural controls, so tend to make the most of what they have. You may have to identify their needs by drawing them out through genuine caring and questioning. They seldom voluntarily go to counsellors, as that would be admitting that they can't handle their own problems. The Buddhist mentality suggests that if one's mind can't keep control, the person is a failure. Since harmony is a key value in Buddhism, one must be careful not to lose face or bring shame on the family, so they try to avoid confrontation – quite the opposite of Western responses. It is wise not to pressure Buddhists into making decisions or to push them to accept Christ. Let the Spirit lay the foundation and rely on friendships for discerning the ripeness of such things. Therefore it takes a longer time to truly build trusting relationships with Asian Buddhists.

Motivations

New arrivals from the East to the West have major adjustments to deal with including language, climate (imagine coming from the tropics to blizzards), culture values and practical daily living. Some arrive as refugees due to war, violence and turmoil in their homelands. These have already suffered a great deal; but even those choosing to come and live in the West face grief, loneliness, the loss of familiar surroundings, family and friends and massive culture shock.

The aspirations of Asian immigrants are to live in peace and freedom, to find productive work and a sound economy for their families, to get a good education for their children, and to experience spiritual openness, sometimes in contrast to the religious confines in their home countries. Many in this situation may feel some disillusionment towards Buddhism; that their calling on the Buddha and the spirit forces was futile and ineffective. They desire a good life and good friends. Along with these aspirations is an ideal view of the West where they expect children to be loved and safe, life to be sacred and respected. They anticipate general morals and standards to be high, all white people to be rich Christians, and, of course, prosperity for all, in a flourishing land of plenty.

Status and Fears

Often Asian refugees and sometimes foreign students come from tribal or slum areas and because their home cultures work quite hierarchically, they are used to knowing their place in specific age and status groups. Consequently, in their newly adopted host lands where everyone is 'equal', they face hesitant and apprehensive feelings of suspicion over the motives of Westerners. They also experience loneliness and homesickness. Beside that there is frustration in communications as they misunderstand and are misunderstood. They feel discouraged and depressed over the enormous adjustments they must make quickly, and fear being exploited all round. Added to this is apprehension and suspicion of the law, particularly of police and military personnel, as many will have had bad experiences in their homelands. It takes time for them to experience and believe that these guardians of society are valuable to them and are there to help them, not abuse them.

Expectations

Ideals can work against them, particularly when those in the West do not fully understand them. After the initial honeymoon period when everything is new and exciting, a time of facing reality and disillusionment may follow within a few months. Their penchant to be reserved and docile, polite and shy, to save face and avoid confrontation may frustrate them in the aggressive West. Their desire to please us so as to be accepted, and to live life in their normal slow pace – not the fast lane of the West – only adds confusion and conflict during their acculturation to the West. Westerners also need to understand that when they say 'yes' that may be purely politeness, or their desire not to offend. They want to help us so they tell us what they think we want to hear, and will not think this is lying.

To alleviate culture shock first-generation Asian immigrants or refugees tend to gravitate to areas in the Western host country where their own kind of people are living. Under pressures of being frequently misinterpreted by Westerners, they may do this in order to gain quicker acceptance and find more comfortable integration. We need to be most sensitive to Asian cultural understandings to help smooth transitions.

Westerners have vital roles to help Asian immigrants and refugees get settled in especially in the early months after arrival. The best models I know of are a couple who have loved and shared their lives with 'foreigners coming to the West' for decades. As Asian students or immigrants arrive they meet them at the airport if possible, help them get settled on campuses, and visit them regularly in college dormitories. They help them adjust to Western culture and become genuine friends. They help them in practical ways like showing them how to go to the bank, where to buy food, how to get drivers' licences, where to post letters, and how the public transportation systems work, giving bus schedules to them and other practical information. They have deep concern for them, advising them on appropriate dress for the climate, teaching them how to speak practical English, helping them fill out forms and papers, taking them to shopping areas and explaining everyday Western activities. Inviting them into homes for meals, transporting them to events, having them to a holiday celebration, and accompanying them on outings can help cement relationships with new arrivals. Acceptance, friendship, empathy, genuine caring and selfless love are the keys to building good relationships. Asian people, like any others, respond with respect, thankfulness and lifelong interest. In that context the lives of Christian witnesses and their natural sharing about Christ has a marked impact. Pure motives back up true models of serving humanity and living the gospel message. We are to love them genuinely, whether or not they accept Christ.

It will obviously be easier to build relationships with Caucasian Buddhists in the West, but we still need to be sensitive to their religious conceptual framework. Some urban populations today, even in 'Buddhist countries', may not be so much Buddhist as secularist and materialist. Nevertheless, the underlying Buddhist assumptions will be similar and do continue to affect their view of the world.

Five

BUDDHISM AND CHRISTIANITY

The Church and Buddhist Culture

Christian encounter with Buddhists can be traced a long way back to the Nestorian period. Richard Garbe[1] estimates, 'Christian influence on Buddhism in Tibet and China has been possible since A.D. 635.' Actually, some five centuries before that, Christians travelled the Silk Road and witnessed in West China, where they established congregations among Buddhists there.

Despite continual Christian interaction with Buddhists since that time, early Roman Catholic missions and later Protestant ones produced only meagre results in church growth. In fact some of the earlier missions to Buddhist peoples in Asia did not even survive.

From the early Nestorians' outreach to Ceylon (A.D. 537) and to China (by A.D. 635), Christian missions faced strong resistance. Usually less than one per cent became Christian. South Korea is one

---

1. Garbe, R. *India and Christendom*. Illinois: The Open Court Publishing Co., 1959: p. 176

notable exception, though over two-thirds of that country is still under Buddhist influence. Christian outreach in Buddhist lands is like slicing a sword through water; even immediately after there is no perceptible impression.

Issues Affecting Buddhist Seekers

The Christian church among Mahayana and Theravada Buddhist communities is a tiny minority, usually less than one per cent of the population with a few rare exceptions. The gospel has remained in the minority in these Buddhist nations.

Three main causes account for the lack of permanent self-perpetuating Christian communities among Buddhist peoples: persecution, syncretism, and the failure of the church to break through the social solidarity of Buddhism. Today these barriers still pose basic problems for Christians seeking to reach out to Buddhists.

Social Solidarity

One major barrier to the spread of Christianity through Buddhist communities is that the national and religious identities of people in Buddhist countries are so interrelated that they are often seen as one and the same. For example, being a Lao means being a Buddhist. Those who choose to become Christians receive enormous pressure to revert to the old religion. Strong family and community influences, and in some cases physical pressure, are brought to bear.

In many Eastern cultures, shame is particularly powerful. Individuals will make every effort to avoid personal shame, or cause another to 'lose face'. A Japanese saying hits the mark: 'The nail that sticks up will be pounded down.' Anyone daring to stand out as a Christian in such communities is likely to face serious opposition from family, friends and society.

In these cultures it takes a lot of strength to go against the grain. It is not unusual for work promotions or incentives to be withheld, especially for Christian government workers. Christians are also often pressured to participate in religious festivals and rites. When reaching out to Buddhists, it is important that whole families are brought to Christ rather than just gathering individuals; a family is more likely to stand together and remain strong despite pressure.

Identity and Belonging

In Asia the group gives meaning to the individual. In the individualistic West the opposite is true. Asians long to conform and belong rather than stick out like a sore thumb or be seen as different. In religious matters, this is even more pronounced, where being Christian is often identified as Western and as rejecting your heritage. It is much easier for Buddhist-background believers if they come to faith with their family. It is also important for new believers to find a strong identity in Christian fellowships. The more the church fits into the local culture and customs, the quicker belonging is established.

Relevant Christianity

To penetrate the barriers of social resistance, the church needs to communicate Christ in a way that is accessible to Buddhists and relevant to their cultures,

Two specific areas to consider are:

1. Ethnotheology – the idea of biblical interpretation and application of Christian beliefs in a way that is culturally significant and accessible.
2. Evangelistic theology and strategy appropriate to the social dynamics and background of the specific people group.

Christianity must not be a foreign appendage or an insular alternative community, which fails to communicate Christ effectively, both by word and works to Buddhist neighbours. The more the church is seen in the everyday things of life, the quicker its relevance is recognized.

Comparing Buddhism and Christianity

Recognising some historical and doctrinal similarities between Christianity and Buddhism, many think they are much the same. For example, the Ten Commandments and the Buddhist Sila (prohibitions) have similar tenets. But be warned, precise meanings and definitions of the concepts and principles compared can be very varied.

Meaning discrepancy is a serious semantic problem for both Buddhists and Christians. The use of similar words does not indicate identical meanings. Even the same symbols may have very divergent interpretations and connotations. For example, some Buddhist scholars like Buddhadasa say Buddhists believe in God. But he interpreted God as equivalent to karma (cause and effect). He also identified God as ignorance; the source of suffering.[2] Neither karma nor ignorance is an accurate equivalent for the true meaning of the personal, holy, omnipotent, living God of the Bible. For those engaged in discussion, dialogue or debate with Buddhists, careful identification of meaning will be crucial. Not being on the same page guarantees failure and misunderstanding.

The contradictions between Buddhism and Christianity are glaring and significant. Certainly Buddhists model examples for the church in maintaining discipline within the clergy and in defending high standards of tradition in their fundamental teachings. They discern deviant and divergent doctrine and discipline those who exceed acceptable limits. Though Christians may agree with some of the actions of Buddhists, there are vital distinctions in crucial motivating beliefs that leave Buddhism and Christianity diametrically opposed.

The following is a true story, though the men's names have been changed...

Some years ago I met Mr Tawd, an elderly gentleman who had been a Buddhist priest for twenty years before he became a Christian. He was born in a small Buddhist village in Burma. There were no schools in the village, so he went to the Buddhist monastery for education for about ten years.

---

2.   Indapanno, Bikkhu Buddhadasa. *Christianity and Buddhism*, Bangkok, Sinclair Thompson Memorial Lectures, fifth series, 1967, pp. 66-7

After this, Tawd went into the Buddhist temple as a novice for five years, and then went on to be a full Buddhist monk for the next fifteen years of his life. In order to gain a bachelor's degree in Buddhism, he left his village. As he studied in the Buddhist University, Tawd diligently progressed as high as he could.

The Buddhist leaders in the Sangha recognized his ability as a lecturer, so sent him to many cities and towns throughout the country to lecture on Buddhism.

One day he went to teach in a certain town where many of the people spoke English. Since he could not speak English fluently, Tawd, the monk, decided he would learn English so that he could speak with the people in that area about Buddhism. He found that the only qualified teacher to help him with English was a Christian who was pastoring a small church in the town without pay. His name was Mr Thom.

In time Tawd approached Thom and asked if he would teach him English. Pastor Thom said he would be glad to do so, but that he had two conditions. First, Tawd would have to meet with him every day for an hour between 8:00 a.m. and 9:00 a.m. This gave the pastor repeated contact with Tawd. Secondly, Thom said they would need a textbook, and the text they would use would be the New Testament in English. The pastor understood that the Word of God would eventually speak for itself. Tawd accepted these two conditions.

For six months Tawd studied daily with Thom so he could spread Buddhism among the English speakers there. But after some time he came across John 14:6: 'I am the way the truth and the life. No one comes to

the father except through me'. Tawd was confused.
The Buddha only claimed to point the way, but Jesus
said he actually was the way! The Buddha said, light
arose within him, but Jesus declared, 'I am the light
of the world.' The Buddha said he learnt truth by self-
intuition, but Jesus affirmed, 'I am the truth.'

These questions challenged Tawd day and night.
The 'I ams' of Jesus contrasted with the 'I knows' of
the Buddha. What was the truth about the Truth?

Slowly, through the study of the Bible and
discussions with the pastor, the light dawned upon
Tawd. He became motivated to change and after some
time left the Buddhist priesthood and accepted Christ.

Tawd explained to me that the Buddha's philosophy was so rich and full of good teaching, but it ques-
tioned God. The Buddhist scholars did not believe
in Creator God, so Tawd's dilemma was centred on
'no God' versus the God of the Bible. The Buddha
himself claimed he was 'omnisense' (self-knowing).
As Tawd meditated on the Bible he began to discover
God as creator, sustainer and Saviour. He already
felt that human merit could not fulfil the demands of
karma. He had faithfully done lots of practise of the
227 rules to follow as a Buddhist priest, but still felt
unfulfilled. These were just the basic laws, and there
were thousands of rules to follow on the way to 'purity.' How could he fulfil all of those? It was impossible
and hopeless. Tawd concluded that in Buddhism the
future was not sure, and that there was not much hope
of attaining nirvana either.

In contrast, Jesus said, 'You are my witnesses.'
Here was present assurance and hope. Tawd suddenly

realized that hope and true life were to be found only in Christ. In this Saviour are all the promises of God. This added double joy. Tawd did not reject the good parts of the teaching of Buddha, but recognized that Buddha had only part of the truth and part of the light, because Buddha himself was searching for truth. He believed that by discovering Christ in relationship to God's revelation, he had found the truth. In Buddhism the merits leading to twenty heavens and the demerits leading to many hells were to be contrasted with God's grace provided in Christ received freely by faith alone. Certainly, karma is a judge, but karma and merit cannot balance each other out, Tawd argued.

Today Tawd is very elderly but still teaching young Christians how to relate to and witness to their Buddhist neighbours, friends and families. The grace of God's gospel is still the 'power of God unto salvation to everyone who believes' (Rom. 1:16).

Six

COMMUNICATING WITH THE BUDDHIST MINDSET

Obstacles to Understanding the Gospel

Some fundamental Buddhist beliefs can make it difficult for Buddhists to grasp the gospel. Examples include:

All Religions Are Valid

Because of the assumed similarity between some of the teachings, some assume that all religions are acceptable. So following Buddhism will have the same result as faith in Christ; whatever will help you with your problems being the important factor. The difficulty with such suggestions is that Buddhists do not believe in God or the salvation He provided in Christ. Furthermore the Buddha emphatically denied he was a god. Also the Buddha clearly affirmed that he could not help anyone. He emphasized that each person must depend only on oneself. Buddhism simply cannot be valid if Christianity is, and vice versa.

There is No God

Buddhism denies the biblical concept of a supreme personal God, the Creator of all, who exists outside of His creation and who, in power and glory, brought all things into being. Buddhism teaches that everything is connected or interdependent; nothing exists separately except as illusion, and everything is in a state of flux, ever changing, and nothing is permanent, so God cannot exist outside and separately from Creation, nor be eternal and always the same.

All supernatural beings, including angels, demons and all gods, were seen by Buddha as insignificant in the quest for nirvana, as all of them are still in the process of rebirth in dealing with karma.

Many of the Thai students I have interacted with have declared that if I could show them God then they would believe in Jesus. Pressing them as to whether things that cannot be seen, such as the scent of a rose, or electricity, actually exist, gave them food for thought. Their attempts to describe them were inadequate. Humans cannot see the spirit world, but just because we can't see God with our naked eyes does not mean He is not real. Evidence in nature all around us, with its order and systems of the universes, as well as those of our human bodies, affirms the need for an intelligent Creator God. Read and study Genesis 1 and 2 with Acts 17:24-25, Colossians 1:15-18, Hebrews 11:3.

Christ is Not God

While the Bible teaches that Christ was fully God and fully man, Buddhists have misunderstood this doctrine and believe Jesus was just a human, who is entirely impotent to help anyone reach nirvana.

The Bible says Christ is the Son of God, the only sinless being suitable or qualified to be the Saviour of the world. Though He was tempted in all points like us, He was without sin (Heb. 4:15).

Often I have asked my Buddhist friends who they thought Jesus was. Replies included: a good man, a prophet, the founder of the Christian religion, and surprisingly, the younger brother of the Buddha! They do not say He was God, the Son of God, an eternal being, or the Creator. The concept of Christ's deity is not understood in Buddhism. Some Buddhist scholars consider the Word (*logos* – John 1:1-3) might be compared to their *Dharma* (word of teaching) or the *Tao* (the way in Chinese philosophy).

One primary starting point for discussion with Buddhist friends concerning Christ as Creator God is John 1:1-5,10. This speaks of Christ as the creator and source of all life, and the light in each human, which helps counteract much misconception.

Christ's miracles and wonders also indicate His connection with the Creator Lord of the universe. His walking on water and facing the storm suggests His power and control over the forces of nature. 'Even the wind and the sea obey Him.'[1]

A discussion on Colossians 1:13-23 might also elucidate Christ's deity. Buddhists may come to understand who God and His divine Christ are in order to comprehend the essence of the gospel. Only in the light of who Christ is, does God's 'sending his only son' make any sense (John 3:16). Christians often start sharing the gospel with a reference to God. This or anything else which starts with 'God',

1.   Mark 4: 35-41; Matthew 14:25-33

will not usually be understood by their hearers in the framework of Buddhist worldview, which excludes any concept of Creator God.

Man is Not a Spiritual Being

The Bible teaches that man and woman were 'made in the image of God'. When God breathed the breath of life into humans each became a living soul (Gen. 2:7). All members of the human race are spiritual beings, possessing a precious eternal quality. Humans are living souls with personality, value and dignity. When Jesus raised Jairus' daughter, 'her spirit returned' (Luke 8:41-42; 49-55). Belief in Christ regenerates the soul in the present, brings rich fulfilment to being, and gives true meaning to spiritual life now, as well as eternal hope for the future.

The Buddha taught the doctrine of *anatta* or 'no-soul, no-ego, no-self.' He rejected the idea of humans having eternal souls, being living spirits or possessing lasting personalities or essence. To him, people were impermanent and transitory, ever facing the problem of how to escape from suffering. All life is meaningless, he said. For Buddhists this may make the idea of God-given purpose and identity hard to appreciate.

Mahayana Buddhism also interprets *anatta* as the Doctrine of *Sunyatta* or emptiness. Rejecting the essential Hindu belief in 'the transmigration of the soul' after death, the Buddha taught that at death the five components (*skandhas*) of human personality dissipated into the greater whole, without any continuing soul or spirit. There the accumulated karma produces rebirth apart from soul. Some say the habits are reborn in the next life. This no-soul *anatta* teaching has produced some conflict among the monks, because some still believe in some kind of soul entity. However, the Sangha (Buddhist community) proscribes those who hold this view and affirms the 'no-soul' fundamental doctrine .

Karma is the Iron Law

In Buddhism karma, rebirth and suffering are inescapable. This can lead to fatalistic attitudes, whereas Christ's gospel offers hope, salvation and optimism for both present and future, even in the midst of suffering.

I remember working with Tong Yu, an elderly leprosy patient in Thailand. As a Buddhist he believed that in previous incarnations he must have been extremely bad to have contracted such a dreadful disease. Because he lost toes and fingers and even much of his nose to leprosy, he had given up on life and just wanted to die. Then some Christians contacted, treated and witnessed to him. He later accepted Christ, was rehabilitated and given a livelihood. He served as a fruitful evangelist and an energetic pastor for about three decades. The power of Christ brought positive changes to his life and released Tong Yu from his supposed karma.

In Buddhist cultures, when children are born with serious defects or suffer tragic accidents, it is not unusual for parents to abandon them at temples or hospitals, believing the child's bad karma from a previous existence had caused such effects.

Reflection on John 9 and the question of what sin was behind the man's blindness, shows that Jesus rejected any previous sin, or 'karma', as the cause, either in the man or his parents.

Jesus also declared that the Galileans whose blood Pilate mingled with their sacrifices were not greater sinners than all the other Galileans, because they suffered that fate. Nor were the eighteen people killed when the Tower of Siloam fell on them worse culprits than all who lived in Jerusalem (Luke 13:1-5). By this argument Christ rejected karma as a system of cause and effect. Instead he showed that all peoples, however they behaved, were levelled to the same plane, all being equal sinners in God's sight; all have come short of the glory of God. Breaking one of the commandments is failure equal to breaking all of them. Moving from the Buddhist reward system to the Christian message of Grace will require a big shift in the individuals thinking.

Sin Has Little Consequence

Both Christianity and Buddhism teach basic morality. Buddha's Five Sila (morality) parallel the latter five of the Ten Commandments (obviously omitting the first five of the commandments that relate to relationship with God). But the concepts of sin in the two religions stand in confused contrast.

I vividly remember a devout Thai Buddhist woman once saying to me, 'I have never sinned.' Buddhists believe humans are basically good and do not have a sinful nature. They would not acknowledge that humans are in rebellion against God. To Buddhists who deny the existence of Creator God, sin does not have any consequences before a holy God. Buddhists are accountable only to themselves and their own karma, as opposed to Christian thinking of sin as rebellion against God.

Buddhist doctrine does not define sin precisely, because existence with its suffering is like sin to them. Sin is the effect of one's *karma*. Buddhists sometimes define sin as

- unwholesome actions (*kamma*),
- desire-craving that turns one away from the Eightfold Path,
- transitory deception (ignorance of the fact that nothing is real, everything is impermanence and emptiness).

In terms of reality, sin is basically illusionary, or an action of incompleteness and ignorance of reality, though the karmic consequences of it will accumulate for those who fail to break the endless cycles of rebirth.

In Buddhist understanding sin may be compared to an axle out of kilter needing repair, or a dislocated joint requiring correction The wicked man is seen as ignorant, needing instruction not punishment. Popularly, Buddhist 'sin' is killing life in any form. Some strict monks sweep the path ahead of them as they walk, to avoid killing tiny life forms.

The Bible identifies sin as a principle in all humankind, a consequence resulting from the Fall of the first created couple in the Garden of Eden. This fatal flaw caused death to come upon all people. Sins are violations of God's character, an affront to Him, failing to maintain His holy standards.

Most Buddhists try to practice the five basic laws or Sila, but karma always has its undeniable, inescapable impact. Buddhists will often keep the Sila for a limited number of days, or around special festivals, but ignore them the rest of the time. Giving consideration to the Buddhist Sila and Buddhists' failure to maintain them fully may be sufficient to raise their awareness of the Christian concept of sin.

Salvation is by Your Own Effort

The means of salvation – faith or works, divine grace or karmic merit, divine provision or self-effort?

Buddha basically taught that individuals have the ability to free themselves from the cycle of life with its deceptive illusion, desires and suffering, and thereby attain a state of perfect non-existence, without the help of God.

As Christmas Humphreys, a notable British convert to Buddhism, emphasized in his writings, the first principle of Buddhism is that self-salvation is the immediate task for all. In Buddhism, no saviour exists. In fact, the Buddha said that even he could not help anyone; he could only point the way. Each person must find their own way to release from the cycle of life. You must deliver yourself. Reaching nirvana relies completely on one's own effort. Overcoming karma must be through self-effort alone, without help from gods or other saviours.

Buddhists attempt self-deliverance through doing good works and making merit. It is important to note, though, that merit does not cancel out bad deeds. Bad deeds will work themselves through just as good deeds will. Buddhists just hope to have more good deeds than bad.

Buddhism projects human thinking out to the infinite, explaining ultimate meanings through their limited human experience and existential awareness. Ancient societies did the same, creating idols as gods from their human knowledge and limited observation.

To the Christian, salvation is possible only through the grace of God in the provision of Christ. Christianity stems from God's condescension to the human level and making Himself known to humankind, rather than in man's ability to understand the infinite supreme God. This divine revelation climaxed in the incarnation of our Lord Jesus Christ, in His voluntary sacrifice, miraculous resurrection and glorious ascension. The gospel of the redemption of humankind through His vicarious sacrifice in our place is therefore unique. It speaks of a transcendent God, revealing Himself in terms of man's own culture and language, and providing a way for reconciling fallen humanity to Himself. The Father sent the Son to be the Saviour of the world (1 John 4:14).

Because the concept of substitution is lacking in the teaching of Buddhism, it is difficult for Christians to communicate this and for Buddhists to comprehend Christ's substitutionary death.

This poses a major problem in sharing Christ's message with Buddhist peoples. In my experience, the following illustration from Thai folklore helps portray the meaning of substitution and its effect. This illustration is extremely helpful in explaining substitution.

Long ago, a king from the south besieged the city of the king of Chiang Mai in the north. Rather than see the city and its residents destroyed, the two kings agreed to select one man each for a contest to see who could stay under water the longest. Terms of this trial by ordeal were set. The two men dived into the river. The first to emerge was the man from the south. Freedom and salvation for the people of Chiang Mai was assured. When the north's man did not come up, the Thai king sent men in to search for him. They found he had tied himself with his sarong (*pha*) to a tree limb under the water so he would not break the water's surface. He deliberately sacrificed his life to save the lives of all in the city. Chedi Khao on the bank of the River Ping still stands to commemorate the man's sacrifice.

The Nature of Life

An important contrast between Buddhism and Christianity is that of final destiny. The ultimate 'hope' in Buddhism is death or extinction, a 'blowing out of the candle of life'. This cessation of existence is nirvana, a term even Buddhist scholars find difficult to define precisely. Nirvana allegedly brings liberation from the endless cycles of rebirth, a release from suffering and worldly engagement, the ending of illusion, impermanence, desire and craving. This belief can make it very hard for Buddhists to grasp the 'good news' of eternal life.

Nirvana is not a heaven or paradise – in Buddhist cosmology these are still types of sensual existence from which even gods and devas must experience more rebirths. Once an individual reaches nirvana, there is no further resurrection either within or out of nirvana, which is a state not part of the physical world. Until that state is reached, Buddhists continue in the circle of life, from death through multiple rebirths, without permanent soul, essence or personality. This is in stark contrast to the Christian concept of heaven that is a place of eternal and abundant life or existence, but without suffering of any kind.

D.T. Niles, a world-renowned ecumenical leader from Sri Lanka[2], brilliantly clarifies the basic Buddhist doctrines of *anicca* (impermanence), *anatta* (no-self), and *dukkha* (suffering) in relation to Christian thinking:

> 'If we do not start with God we shall not end with him, and when we start with him we do not end with the doctrines of *anicca*, *anatta* and *dukkha*.

> 'The existence of God means the existence of an order of life which is eternal – *nicca*[3] (permanence). It means that there is for the soul an identity which is guarded by God's sovereignty and remains through eternity – *atta*. Within this context, sorrow – *dukkha* – is seen to consist, not so much in the impermanence of things, as in the perverseness of our wills which seek these things instead of the things which are eternal.

---

2. Niles, D.T. *Buddhism and the Claims of Christ*. Richmond Virginia: John Knox Press, 1967: p. 27
3. In Pali, the prefix 'a' negates, meaning 'not'

'The circle of the Christian faith can thus be
described as that which starting with God leads
man to the realisation that God alone affords
the most adequate base for a most meaningful
explanation of life's most significant facts.'

Buddha saw life was meaningless in itself and set
out to rescue men from this meaninglessness. Jesus
proclaimed that life was meaningful in God, and set
out to call men to share that meaning (John 10:10).

Furthermore, in Buddhism, death is the final
category.[4] In the gospel, the final category is life.
Buddhists seek to shorten life, to escape from the
never-ending cycle of rebirths. The gospel emphasizes
everlasting life (John 3:16-18; 11:25-26). In Christ
the finality is eternal life to be enjoyed forever in
heaven with Creator God following the resurrection
of all (John 14:1-5).

Altruism and Compassion

True Christianity is centred in altruism not selfishness.
Christ is the supreme model, giving His life for all
humankind. Buddhist karma encourages preoccupation
with self-dependence, so essentially it is highly
individualistic and tends to become self-centred. The
ultimate goal may be that each one, as part of the greater
whole, will contribute to the liberation of all, but day-to-
day it focuses on one's self.

Although societies have group functions, Buddhism
demands that the individual alone works out his/her

---

4.   Niles 1967: pp. 29, 34, 35

own salvation; overcoming karma, and freeing one's self from the cycle of life. In this respect Buddhism is oriented around self and not the group. Socially the Asian group gives meaning to the individual, but religiously the central drive of Buddhism is individual self-deliverance. This obsessive spiritual preoccupation focuses each person's energies on his or her own release from karma, suffering and Samsara. This social difference is significant – the Buddhist social order is dominated by the individual, and there is a lack of sense of relation, man to man, and man to God.[5] In Thailand, for instance, it is almost inconceivable for Thai Buddhists to believe that the Christian missionary has come out of selfless concern for them without an incentive for personal gain. They often ask the question, 'What are you getting out of this – a higher salary? Government sponsorship? More merit?' This can often undermine our attempts to show love and compassion, and make it hard for Buddhists to grasp Jesus' sacrifice.

To the Christian the way up is down; taking the servant role, pouring oneself out as a drink offering to fellow humans. To Buddhists, the way up is a self-centred preoccupation. To use others for your advancement may be acceptable. After all, karma conditions and causes people to be in their current state. Of course it is noted that many, including some Christians, tend to exhibit similar selfish attitudes, but these are contrary to the biblical gospel.

---

5.   Eakin, Paul A. *Buddhism and the Christian Approach to Buddhists in Thailand*. Bangkok: R. Hongladaromp, Printer & Publisher, 1956: pp. 56, 63

The first Noble Truth states plainly that the whole world is suffering. Though some Buddhist groups are developing compassionate aid agencies, and Mahayana Buddhists recognise Avalokiteshvara (Kwan Yin) as the bodhisattva of compassion, most Buddhist talk of suffering is more like an intellectual awareness of the results of karma, rather than an expression of loving compassion for others that Christ demonstrates. The more Christians practise genuine care, merciful concern and loving compassion, the more our Buddhist friends will want to find out why we do so.

Loving service can be a powerful relational connector and conversation starter.

Merit or Grace

Another major difference is the principle of salvation, or ultimate attainment. For Buddhists, self-effort and 'boot-strap' deliverance through their own human energies and abilities is a cardinal principle. Depend only on yourself.

Buddhists believe that by 'making merit' they will overcome their karma and so move towards enlightenment. Buddhists make merit in scores of ways such as doing good works or giving food to the monks. Devotees can also 'transfer merit' to parents by becoming monks, or to their ancestors through special ceremonies. In Mahayana Buddhism, bodhisattvas are enlightened beings who delay their going to nirvana in order to use their merit to help others reach enlightenment.

The gospel, by contrast, declares that dependence on self and confidence in the flesh spells doom. We are utterly helpless apart from the grace of God in Christ alone. Salvation comes through dependence on Almighty God. It is operational through the believer's faith in Christ and His grace (Eph. 2:8-9, Gal. 2:20, 3:7, Rom. 3:28, 4:1-25).

If merit can be earned by human effort alone, God's grace and the forgiveness Christ provided on the cross are not needed. Earning merit and receiving grace are not the same. Salvation, according to the Bible, does not depend on man's efforts (Eph. 2:7-9). Christ's grace is freely given. Consider the ability of humans to keep the Sila, or Buddhist laws, perfectly. It's impossible. Christ was the only perfect human (John 1:14) who had no karma to 'cancel out'. Jesus proclaimed, 'which of you convinces me of sin?' (John 8:46).

The Buddhist idea of karma can tend towards fatalism, hopelessness, self-excusing and pessimism. Buddhism has no possibility of forgiveness; Karma is the iron law to which there is no exception.[6]

Contrast this with the gospel of the loving God who gives forgiveness, mercy, hope, and an exchanged life. Christ's atoning sacrifice is sufficient, providing cleansing from the past, power in the present, and hope for the future.

Scriptures

Buddhists believe the Buddha intuitively realized the teachings he then espoused. On the Buddha's death, in order to ensure the accurate preservation of this

6.   Appleton, George. *The Christian Approach to the Buddhist*. London: Edinburgh House Press, 1958: p. 52

teaching, a group of monks met, at the First Buddhist Council. All the Buddha's teachings were recalled and the *Vinaya*, or disciplines, recited. The *Vinaya* – which became the list of behaviours to be followed by the Sangha – was formally approved and accepted as canonical.

Christianity is based on the divine revelation of God's Word in Scripture. Buddhist texts do not claim to be inspired in the way the Bible is. But followers still highly esteem and respect the *Tripitaka* (Three Baskets), the Pali Canon of Theravada Buddhism, and the Sutras of Mahayana Buddhism. The Biblical Canon is closed, but the Buddhist Sutras are still open and have been added to from time to time.

It is obvious that many differences exist between Buddhism and Christianity – some significant issues being diametrically opposed. Some things may seem similar, but when these concepts are precisely defined they are found to be poles apart.

Seven

SHARING THE GOSPEL

Communicating Christ to Buddhists

Witnessing is never easy. The better the relationships are built with a person, the easier it is to share openly with them. Communicating is still often difficult, but the relationship is essential to spreading the good news.

In today's pluralistic climate, learning how to live and share the gospel with others of differing viewpoints is important. To do so without sacrificing personal convictions or compromising Christian standards takes much patience, charity, understanding and tact. This especially relates to passing on our Christian faith to Buddhists. I suggest three practical actions for consideration.

First, Clarify Essential Concepts

Productive witness requires effective communication. Thai culture, like that of many Asian peoples, is deeply steeped in Buddhism. The religious and educational language is heavily infiltrated with Buddhist terms, connotations and concepts. For centuries, the gospel has established a Christian moral base in many Western nations. Buddhism likewise tied together the fragmented peoples of Asia, particularly those animistic populations, and became the basis of morality, social behaviour and education. This religious overlay forms the framework or grid in which communication takes place. Consider some of the hindrances to communication in this environment.

Much misunderstanding about the definition and meanings of religious terms and concepts exists among Christians and Buddhists. Often terms are falsely considered as equivalent to each other. Patient discussion may help clarify these foundational beliefs.

Christians must clearly explain the meanings of key concepts that are most difficult for Buddhists to comprehend or accept. Using analogies, stories and illustration as skylights for understanding, along with relevant Scripture, helps immensely. Here are some concepts you may wish to clarify. Use the verses below to come up with a Christian definition of each term.

1. The Universe

Is the world a concrete reality or just a transitory illusion from which we need to detach ourselves and escape?

   Consider: Malachi 3:6; Revelation 14:6-7; 2 Peter 3:3-6.

2. God

Is God transcendent, the creator of the universe and personally involved in His creation, or just a controller, an impersonal void or nothingness?

   Consider: Ecclesiastes 12:7-13; Colossians 1:15-18.

3. Christ

Was Christ a unique and sacrificial redeemer, both fully God and fully man, or just a human?

   Consider: Matthew 16:16-17; John 5:18-24; 8:58.

4. Man

Are people made with a spirit, that exists eternally and distinct from all other people, or are men only karmic recycling or matter, impermanent, non-distinct and lacking any form of soul or spirit?

Consider: Genesis 1:26-27; 2:7; Matthew 10:28; 11:29.

5. Sin

Is sin our rebellious natures and selfish acts that affront holy God or merely illusion, ignorance or killing life?

Consider: Isaiah 53:6; John 8:34; Romans 3:9-10.

6. Grace

Is grace freely bestowed through Christ or must we work, with human effort, under the law of karma to receive any reward?

Consider: Ephesians 2:8-9; Acts 4:12; John 1:17-18.

7. Salvation

Does Christ's substitutionary death on the cross provide a way for our salvation, or are we cycling round an unrelenting circle of death and rebirth, driven by karma?

Consider: John 3:16-18; Romans 3:25-26; 5:9; Ephesians 1:7-8; Hebrews 9:12-14; 26-28; 2 Corinthians 5:21.

8. Life

Are people regenerated through spiritual new birth by faith, or simply reincarnated to work out accumulated karmic consequences?

Consider: John 3:3-8; 1 Peter 3:18; Titus 3:5.

9. Heaven

Is heaven the place of eternal resurrected life or virtual extinction, a release from existence into nirvana?

Consider: John 5:29, 11:24-26; Romans 6:3-10; 2 Peter 3:3-5.

> It's important to remember that life to Buddhists is suffering. So beginning your gospel explanation with the idea of eternal life, John 3:16 or the like, may be understood by the Buddhist as eternal suffering, and not something to be desired.
>
> Luke's Gospel is a good place to start sharing the Christian faith with Buddhists because of its many parables and references to Old Testament books such as Proverbs, Ecclesiastes, Job and Jeremiah. Luke also presents Jesus as the Prince of Peace — an idea that will appeal to Buddhists.

Second, Check they heard what you meant

Many unwittingly believe that communication is what is said, rather than what is heard. How often we hear, 'What a clear presentation of the gospel,' but the main concern should be how clear was the reception? In cross-cultural settings the terms that Christians use may be identical to the local ones, but usually these local terms are loaded with Buddhist influences, and not necessarily equivalent in meaning at all. For example, the communicator has in mind Christian concepts of sin, heaven, hell, God, faith, but uses words loaded with ideas of karma, self-effort, enlightenment and bodhisattvas. Is it any wonder that Buddhists often reply, 'Oh, if that is Christianity, it is just the same as Buddhism.'

The gospel communicator must remember that he cannot transfer meaning. The Christian may encode the message, but the Buddhist decodes it. Therefore the communicator can only transfer 'bits' of information. The meaning is then formed in the mind of the receiver in terms of his own cultural grid.

The solution is to establish a circle of communication – a feedback mechanism to evaluate real, not perceived, communication. This determines what meaning and message was actually understood. Conversational exchange is best – rather than just 'telling'; listening is a vital part of the process for effective communication. The more interchange and feedback to clarify meaning which occurs, especially through repeated contact, the more likely biblical understanding will be truly perceived.

Nevertheless, while precise communication is the communicator's responsibility, remember it is the Holy Spirit alone who transmits spiritual truth to the heart. At times the Holy Spirit works, despite the ignorance and blunders of the presenter, but this is no excuse for failing to make determined efforts to sharpen the communication of the good news.

Third, Have Confidence

*   Be aware God is working sovereignly in the lives of those He is calling into His church. So trust God to do His work.

*   Be sure that the Holy Spirit is the primary agent for producing conviction and conversion, not the human agent. Only God's Spirit can open blind eyes to see the truth of Christ. So find out where God is working and get alongside.

- Only the powerful Word of God proclaimed, clearly understood, and received by faith can transform lives, families, societies and whole people groups. So meditate on, memorise and share God's Word sensitively, lovingly and appropriately.

- Be faithful in following Christ's model: Jesus 'went about doing good' (Acts 10:38). Only the godly living witness of Christ in Christians can demonstrate God's love and peace to their Buddhist friends and neighbours. So be clear 'living letters about Christ'(2 Cor. 3:3).

- Be available as God's instruments of service. Jonathan Bonk, editor of the International Bulletin of Missionary Research, says, 'Jesus' life was filled with divine interruptions.' These were opportunities to proclaim, to serve, and to heal, even at most inconvenient times. So be ready and prepared to minister always.

- Be hopeful; 'You shall seek me and you shall find me when you search for me with all your heart' (Jer. 29:13). So be expectant and positive.

- Be dependent always on Christ through prayer, obedience, and faith. So intercede faithfully.

Fourth, Practise Love and Patience

- Remember to pray first! Ask God to open minds, hearts and eyes spiritually (John 14:13-14). Request the Lord to give discernment and wisdom, and to bring every thought captive through obedience to Christ.

- Respect the followers of other faiths as human beings whom God created with dignity (John 1:3-4, 9). Do not destroy their faith, but help transfer their faith from the wrong object to the right one, or from a good one to a better one (Acts 26:18).

- Reflect models of the Christian home with good moral and ethical living yourself (2 Cor. 4:1-5).

- Rigorously earn the right to speak – be credible, honest, and loving with crisp integrity and genuine humility (Acts 19:37).

- Recognise that all religions have some good in them. Do not attack the person nor run down anyone's religion. Listen respectfully.

- Reject any attitude to judge, criticise or make fun of another's beliefs. Open up discussion and dialogue with them on why they believe as they do.

- Relate to them in true Christian love and genuine affection. Be good neighbours – truly friendly and genuinely caring. Be genuine friends to them.

- Be ready to share Christ. Give them God's Word as appropriate occasion arises or interest and opportunity affords.

- Resist the temptation to pressure them to believe or to listen to the gospel. Only the Spirit persuades. Serve them sensitively and patiently as opportunity affords. For example, pray for them when they are sick, encourage them in trouble, help them in crisis, love them at all times.

- Rejoice at what God is doing and will do in their lives and families. Believe He is working. Have positive hope in the operation of His sovereign grace. Praise the Lord.

Today's cultural relativism, situational ethics, secularism and humanism are flooding the communicative media. Anti-Christian slogans surround the believer. Much pressure is brought upon Christians to reduce the uniqueness of Christ. The authority of the Bible is attacked. The sufficiency and necessity of the Christian gospel are assailed. Many forces squeeze the church to compromise the faith and reduce it to an 'on-par' level with all other religions. The church is in danger of being swallowed up by a gross deception. Christians, however, must quietly stand against these erroneous suggestions.

A sympathetic understanding of what Buddhists believe and practice is certainly needed. But Christian approaches should always be with humility, loving demeanour and gentle persuasion. The testimony of a dynamic personal relationship with Jesus Christ provides a powerful, living demonstration of the gospel. Everywhere humans of all creeds, colours and cultures are lost in sin, alienated from God their creator. The urgency of life's fragility motivates the church to communicate the gospel to everyone. The effectiveness of Christ's ambassadors will be proportionate to their dependence on the power of the Holy Spirit and their sensitivity to the cultural concepts of those to whom they go.

Eight

APPROACHES TO SHARING THE GOSPEL

Many approaches and methods have been tried in presenting the gospel to Buddhists. No major breakthrough has occurred through the use of any one particular method or strategy. This is not surprising as it is better to tailor the approach to the individual or particular group being reached. Buddhist beliefs vary considerably even within the regions of one country, so we need to be sensitive to this and remember to treat each individual and family with respect. We must love our Buddhist friends and not simply seek to convert them. It is important to sympathetically study and understand another religion, both in terms of respect and effective communication, before seeking to present Christ to its followers. Once we understand our Buddhist friends, we can decide what might be the next most appropriate action to take in guiding them towards Christ.

Here are some different approaches you might use to begin presenting Christ to your Buddhist friends.

The Apologetic Approach

Sometimes comparisons between Buddhism and Christian beliefs can be used to begin discussions. These form the basis of argument to logically lead

Buddhists to better understand the gospel. The apologetic approach can also be valuable in teaching Christians to understand their faith in contrast to the Buddhist way

Boonmi Rungruangwongs, a well-known Thai pastor, argued bluntly about Buddhist ideas in his Thai booklets on God, Desire, and a 22-point rationale for killing animals.[1] He debated these topics in the context of Buddhist thought with arguments relevant to reasoning Buddhist minds.

Theological explanation is important, but we should remember that a living, vibrant faith speaks volumes. Paul Eakin[2], a Christian scholar on Buddhism, affirmed that Buddhists will not understand Christ better or clearer through Buddhist philosophy, so instead of comparing and expounding on Buddhist scriptures, his apologetics focus on two main 'gaps' in Buddhist thinking...

1. A challenge to the traditional Buddhist cosmol-
    ogy, using Genesis to convince them of God as
    Creator of the world including all its life-forms.
    Perhaps following this approach up by asking ques-
    tions on intelligent design might be beneficial.

    If you decide to look at the character of God,
    make sure you do not make the Creator seem
    evil, which is what Buddhist karmic thinking
    suggests. A fresh interpretation counteracting

---

1. These booklets are available from Suriyaban Bookstore of the
    Church of Christ in Thailand.
2. Eakin 1956: pp. 61-62

ignorance (*avijja*) as the cause of suffering must be taught, explaining that it does not originate with the Creator God, but with the rebellious choice of humans; the real source of ignorance and consequent suffering.

2. Understanding salvation through Christ the Redeemer, with the possibility of forgiveness from sin and remission of the penalty or punishment for all rebellion and failure, including the effects of karma. A useful illustration along these lines is exhibited in the revered King of Thailand, who on his birthday, remits certain sentences and frees prisoners from jail. These transgressors are released, with no further punishment to pay for their crimes, and even given money by the government.

Asking Buddhists to explain their cosmology and the many stages of existence might be another topic to discuss. Daniel McGilvary, pioneer missionary to northern Thailand in the nineteenth century, predicted the total eclipse of the sun on August 17, 1868. Explaining the science he used gained him his first convert, Nan Inta, a Buddhist abbot and diligent student of Buddhism. Nan Inta had argued with McGilvary on the science of geography, the shape of the earth, the nature of eclipses, and so on. There is much myth in unfounded scientific concepts in early Buddhist cosmology as there was in early views of other world societies. Finally, when Nan Inta saw the eclipse occur on the date McGilvary predicted, Inta's faith in the old cosmology was shattered. He converted.[3] Today, experimenting with discussions on intelligent design might be worth investigating in our current intellectual climate.

Two other areas that may fit into apologetics are reincarnation and karma. Rebirth is most difficult to prove scientifically and karma as the source of the creation of the universe begs the question of who initiated the karmic cycle. We can raise serious questions on these and similar topics for open, honest interaction.

Wan Petchsongkram, a former Buddhist monk, also likes the apologetic method, and centres his arguments around the person of God and God as creator.[4] He deals with conflicting interpretations on concepts within Buddhism, such as *vinyaan* (soul, spirit) and *nipaan* (*nirvana*).[5]

Searching minds can also ask questions such as; If no soul essence exists, what really is reborn after we die? Is karma the only thing that is recycled? If human soul does not exist, what then is reborn? If humans have no soul or spirit, how then can they be held accountable for karma and its supposed consequences? If no soul exists how is one responsible for one's karma?

The apologetic approach is usually only suitable to use with deeply thinking, educated Buddhists.

3. McGilvary, Daniel. *A Half Century Among the Siamese and the Lao.* New York: Fleming H. Revell Co., 1912: pp.96-97
4. Petchsongkram, Wan. *Talk in the Shade of the Bo Tree*, translated and edited by Frances E. Hudgins. Bangkok: private printing, 1975:pp. 54f, 64f
5. Petchsongkram 1975: pp. 39f, 119f

Most popular or folk Buddhists do not fall into this category, though there are exceptions. And be warned; directly confronting Buddhists on their beliefs will usually produce a defensive, resistant reaction, rather than a positive response. Remember to be sensitive to your Buddhist friends and respect and love them for who they are.

The Point-of-Contact Approach

This approach uses elements in Buddhism as stepping stones towards understanding Christianity. Ethical and moral similarities can be used to begin a discussion. For example, some look at the doctrine of karma, suggesting it deals with an incompleteness that will only find its fulfilment in Christ. The cause and effects of the curse of karma is done away with through Christ's redemption and resurrection.

Within the animistic foundations of many folk Buddhist societies, there are some redemptive analogies that can be used to introduce the work of Christ. An example among Tibetan Buddhists is the practice of using scapegoats to carry away their family problems and diseases. This model has an Old Testament counterpart, which points to Christ.

A successful example of the 'point-of-contact' approach happened in Korea. In 1907, Buddhist Korea experienced a strong Christian movement. One key to Korean church growth was the missionaries' choice of an indigenous name for God: Hananim. Once a year the Korean king would go to an island in the middle of the river near the capital to make special offerings to Hanylnim. This name indicated he was a high, lofty being in heaven. The missionaries used this name, but taught about the true character of the 'being in heaven'. Their knowledge was more intimate and authoritative than the Korean king's, so the people listened intently. This produced a significant turning of thousands of Koreans to Christ. Soon they adopted the name Hananim (Hana = one), a more biblically accurate name for God.

From the long distant past, like many Asian peoples, before Buddhism came, the Thai people believed in some kind of god in terms of a spirit and divine being. This remains in the Thai language; the word *phrachao* (god) is a truly Thai term referring to 'something which one fears and must beseech or flatter, an instinct among all thinking beings.' The *Brahmans* (members of the highest Hindu caste) introduced the concept of the king as an incarnation of god, hence the original word *phrachao* was also used for the king. The Thai word for the personal pronoun 'I' then became *Khaphrachao*, meaning the servant or slave of god or lord. When Buddhism became dominant, there developed a tendency to glorify each king as a Buddha. The first-person pronoun was then changed to *Khaphra-Buddhachao*, which in its present-day use has been abbreviated to *Khapachao*.[6]

Christians should be concerned to find meaningful expressions and culturally appropriate illustrations in order to share the gospel. Look for these historical illustrations, parables and cultural norms in culture. Through them we can often explain spiritual truth.

---

6.   Indapanno, Bhikkhu Buddhadasa. *Christianity and Buddhism*. Bangkok, Sinclair Thompson Memorial Lectures, fifth series, 1967: pp. 61, 63

For example in Thailand, the theological concept of substitution is incongruous with Buddhist religious beliefs. But a beautiful historical illustration of the famous Queen Suriyothai of the Ayuthaya period helps open the windows of understanding on giving one's life for others. Briefly stated, in 1549 the Thai king Chakharaphat went out to fight the opposing Burmese ruler. Queen Suriyothai disguised herself as a Thai warrior and, unbeknown to her royal husband, rode out to the battle. In the ensuing fight the Thai king was losing the advantage. He was about to be cut down. Seeing this, the queen deliberately drove her elephant between the Burmese king and her husband. She was slain by the long-handled knife wielded by the Burmese ruler, but her husband escaped. Realising what had happened, the King later built a special stupa memorial to her in honour of her bravery and sacrifice. The gospel application is obvious. In recent years a full-length film of Queen Suriyothai, one of only four Thai heroines in history, was produced. Every Thai from grade one to university graduate knows this famous story.

Elements such as these lie waiting for Christians to apply them as levers or springboards to share the gospel. Obviously using this approach you need to be careful that Buddhist scriptures are not attributed an accuracy, authority or divine revelation they do not claim and that Christian doctrine is fully understood. Here is an example to think through ...

Among folk Buddhists in Laos and Thailand, the church grew between 1884 and 1914 from 152 to 6,900 members. A number of intertwining factors led to this growth, but one factor appears to have come from a mythical prophecy in the Laos Buddhist books about a future *Maitreya Buddha*. Other Buddhas preceded Gautama and others, including Maitreya, are still to arise. Part of the prophecy about Maitreya says:

> Myriads of ages ago a white crow laid five eggs; each of these eggs was to hatch and bring forth a Buddha; these Buddhas were to appear in the upper world, one by one; four have already appeared; the last is about to come. The people believed that he will be the greatest and best of all; that he will gloriously reign 84,000 years, and that in his time, all men will become pure in heart.[7]

The missionaries used this starting point within the Buddhist culture to bridge the religio-cultural gap in meaningful communication, going on to expound the riches of Christ, as a possible fulfilment of *Maitreya*.

- Could this prophecy be used as a second coming comparative or not?
- Can the concept of this Maitreya Buddha be used as a redemptive analogy fulfilling the first or second coming of Jesus Christ?
- Can it even be used as a point of contact from which to proceed towards the gospel?
- Does equating Christ's coming with the Maitreya grant high revelation to Buddhist scriptures?
- Is being a 'messianic Buddhist' acceptable to either the church or to the Buddhist Sangha?

---

7. Harris, W. 'Unprecedented Opportunity in the Far East,' *Students and the Modern Missionary Crusade*. New York: Student Volunteer Movement for Foreign Missions, 1906: p. 214

Buddhist scholars deny that Christ could be the prophesied *Maitreya Buddha* because the current period is still within the Age (*kulpa*) of Gautama Buddha. Therefore Christ's first coming 2,000 years ago already negates the possibility that Jesus could fulfil the future *Maitreya Buddha*. Since Christ is also the same person who returns in His Second Coming, he cannot be *Maitreya*, because *Maitreya* is not the same as Gautama Buddha.

So how do we give Christianity contextual credibility without slipping into syncretism and compromise?

Contextualising the gospel means looking at the lives and context of the people we are trying to reach and presenting the gospel in a way that they can understand and that fits with their existing culture. This could be anything from dressing a certain way, to using a specific language, or presenting the information in a certain way. For example, in Asian cultures, especially among rural and tribal populations, oral communication tends to predominate. Buddhist cultures are rich and replete with song, dance, drama, music and other arts, and these are an accessible means of communication for many. Basing a Bible study on much reading and personal study, as often happens in the West, would not work well, but scriptural songs, stories and dramas could be much more effective.[8]

The use of stories, parables, symbols and analogies is generally more acceptable to the Buddhist mind

---

8. *Communicating Christ Through Story and Song* by Paul de Neai has some useful ideas. See the resources section for more information.

than well-crafted arguments. The Bible is full of rich parables and illustrations. In telling these stories, don't be tempted to over-explain them instead of letting the meaning shine forth by itself. Parables or analogies are great ways to get Buddhists to open up for discussion and will help them evaluate the gospel's meaning. To many Asians, especially the more traditional, rural people, the Apostle Paul's arguments in strict linear, logic form, such as those in the book of Romans, are difficult to follow. Their minds tend to be conditioned more to contextual-type logic; lots of different situations and stories all pointing to the same truth, similar to the spokes in a wheel pointing to a common hub of meaning. This contextual form is used in the book of Hebrews, so that may be a more helpful place to start studying the Bible with them. Understanding an individual's cultural process of communication will produce more effective witness.

What does Christianity look like from the eyes of a Buddhist-background believer? What do we do that is not necessarily Christian but mostly Western or cultural?

Christians should neither settle for integrative syncretism by welding Buddhism and Christianity together, nor a fully Buddhist-style expression of the gospel. Both would distort the true meaning of the gospel. An expression of the gospel in Buddhist cultures must present the exact truth of God, yet also be clothed in meaningful garb that communicates appropriately to the Buddhist cultural context.

Efficient communication starts within the context of the audience. Selective Buddhist scriptures may be used as starting points, attention get-ers or interest awakeners for sharing the gospel. Using the five Sila to establish a basis for sin and its consequences is an example. Important stories in the sutras also help. For example, one narrative tells of Buddha's cousin who gave his life to save his people. In that narrative the royal cousin whose city was starving under siege, negotiated with the attacking king. The aggressor agreed to let the people come out and get food and drink for as long as the cousin stayed under water. Buddha's cousin dived in and tied his long hair to a tree root, voluntarily drowning so his people could be saved. This suitably illustrates the biblical concept of substitution and sacrifice.

The Shame Approach

Among the face-saving societies of Buddhist Asia, shame rather than guilt is a dominant trait. Guilt is culpability for committing an offence, whereas shame is a feeling of distress, disgrace or intense regret about a situation. People do not necessarily feel guilt for doing something wrong, unless it causes shame.[9]

Interestingly, shame is referred to in Scripture more than guilt. Shame is mentioned almost seven times as much as guilt. Sin and repentance are about shame, rather than just guilt. The gospel message of repentance and forgiveness will be much easier for Asians to understand if it is presented as 'sin-

---

9. Lowell L. Noble's book, *Naked and Not Ashamed*, is an anthropological, biblical and sociological study of shame. He makes some interesting observations on Japan, China and Thailand (1975: pp. 46-63). Joseph R. Cooke's paper 'The Gospel for Thai Ears' also majors on the 'shame' approach.

shame-Saviour', rather than 'sin-guilt-Saviour', as is acceptable in the West. Emphasising shame rather than guilt in Asia is more culturally appropriate and meaningful.

One issue is how to deal with the Buddhist preoccupation with self-salvation. In a 'losing-face' or shame culture, one can feel shame for purely selfish reasons. The issue is to see in one's shame a responsibility to others and particularly to God. The shame approach must overcome the focus purely revolving around self.

At some points shame does have a wider orientation. It affects the whole extended family and a person's circle of friends so that they also feel ashamed. In Asia, honour killing is not unusual for family members to appease the shame an individual brought on the family. Part of the motivation for abandoning a deformed child at a Buddhist temple is shame.

Another matter is how to instil accountability to God, as Buddhists do not believe God exists. Concepts of shame do need to be defined. Shame in the West is not necessarily identical to shame in the East.

The 'Scratch Where It Itches' Approach

If your elbow itches, you don't scratch your head. Yet that is exactly what Christians do when they rigidly proclaim the gospel message without taking into account where people's hurts, felt needs or 'itches' are. Christ always applied His message to the appropriate needs of the individual or group. He was constantly teaching to their need, applying the gospel to precisely where the people hurt. He asked blind Bartimaeus, 'What do you want me to do for you?'(Luke 18:41).

As Henry Otis Dwight[10] pointed out, the large populations under Buddhism and other world religions in their entirety can be daunting, seeming like 'great hostile fortresses.' Rather than trying to challenge an entire community of faith we should look for cracks in the walls, or flaws in the strongholds as 'strategic points for effective evangelism.' By locating smaller areas of responsiveness, rather than the large-scale community, Christians can meet the practical and spiritual needs of families and individuals. These cracks and flaws are to be recognized and healed with gentle love.

Felt needs of Buddhists vary. Naturally, human concerns like survival, family issues and economic sufficiency are common or universal. But the paramount concerns of many popular Buddhists are:

• Fear
  Fear of going to any of the eight levels of Buddhist hells, of being alone, and particularly of losing face or being shamed.

  Many folk Buddhists live in fear of animistic spirits, ancestral ghosts and witchcraft. Many of those who turned from Buddhism to Christ in the early movement in north Thailand and Laos did so to obtain freedom from accusations of witchcraft and the social ostracism associated with it. I met quite a few cases of Buddhists who became

---

10. Dwight, Henry Otis (ed). *The Blue Book of Missions for 1905*. New York: Fung & Wagnalls Co., 1905: pp. 82-83

Christians to be freed from spirit oppression. They had prayed to Buddha and other gods, made offerings to the spirits, worshipped idols, gone into the priesthood, and still had no release. Frustrated, they met Jesus at the point of their need.[11]

• Healing
From sicknesses, diseases and demonic attacks, the alleviation of habitual debt and exorbitant interest, and the resolution of personal conflicts, deep hurts and pressures from within their families.

Many Buddhists who have come to Christ have first come 'to the end of themselves'. Many conversions from Buddhism swing on the pivotal point of the inability to accomplish perfection by oneself or to overcome debilitating weaknesses.

A classic example is the leprosy patients in rural Thailand, with whom I worked. Many had significant deformities from leprosy. They found their social, physical, and spiritual needs met through our medical clinics, acceptance as normal humans and mutual fellowship in churches. Numerous people have turned to Christ because of their contact with Christians in clinics or hospitals.[12]

• Suffering
Above all is the importance of overcoming their own karma and suffering in this present life. Their

---

11. Smith, Alex G. *Strategy to Multiply Rural Churches* (A Central Thailand Case Study). Bangkok: OMF Publishers, 1977: p. 158
12. Smith 1977: p. 173

karma has overplayed itself. They are fed up, hopeless, frustrated and discouraged. Hearing the gospel and seeing Christ's love through His servants helps some to turn to Jesus. Some may also do so out of ulterior motives.

The 150,000 South-East Asian refugees, who arrived in Thailand from nearby Buddhist lands between 1975 and 1980, are an example. At the point of their exasperation and frustration when life was so uncertain, they sought for someone to truly depend on to help them. During much caring ministry the Thai Southern Baptists baptized 2,100 Cambodian and Vietnamese refugees during the three years following 1975. The national crises suffered by some Buddhist countries in recent decades make one wonder whether God allowed them to reach an extremity, to an end of trusting in themselves, in order to steer them towards the gospel of His grace.

These are some 'itches' many face. Christianity needs to be practical in modern ways, not just in the demonstration of good works, but also in applying teachings to the urgent itches and real needs of the people.

Teachers and sharers of God's good news ought to observe carefully and to listen conscientiously to individuals and their communities before trying to step in with the balm of the gospel. Theology divorced from the real needs of people is futile, but so is social service without gospel pronouncement. Remember that Peter provided the crippled beggar of Acts 3 with both the saving name and the helping hand and together these led to the beggar's transformation.

Furthermore, through an incarnational approach of sharing Christ within a community, Christians build credibility. We sit where they sit and feel what they feel, becoming a living demonstration of the gospel and of the empathetic difference Christ makes.

The Power Encounter Approach

Many Buddhists live in fear. Fear of spirits, ghosts, the afterlife, hells, the impact of their karma and its effect on their personal security and prosperity. Presenting Christ as the one who has authority over all these areas can be extremely powerful.

Thai Buddhists have a deep respect for phra, an impersonal, quantitative, supernatural power. Many other beliefs and concepts involve power in holy water, sacred strings, incantations, tattoos, amulets, and miniature phra objects they hang around their necks or other parts of the body (The Thai call these power objects *khryang raang khong khlang*). Most of these relate to the concern for protection, security, and invulnerability, or for power over others especially in economics and love life.

The gospel presents Christ as the superior power over all these elements. The message of power might be presented as follows:

1. God is the original source of all power and perfection. Jesus Christ is the all-powerful Lord. He is Creator and Governor over all beings (John 1:1-3; Col. 1:16-17).

2. God created humans in the image of God, and gave them power to govern the world and care for it. The first human couple was originally perfect and

enjoyed freedom and power in the presence of God
without shame, sin or death (Gen. 1:26-27; 2:7-25).

3. Humans lost that power through their own
    wilful disobedience and rebellion against God.
    The human race then came under the power of
    evil and demonic spirits, resulting in suffering,
    shame and death. Humans thus started the
    process of karma and became slaves to sin
    (Gen. 3; Rom. 5:12; John 8:34; Eph. 2:1-3).

4. Jesus saw humankind had no possible way to free
    themselves from the power of Satan, sin, shame
    and karma. Christ came down to break the power
    of Satan over human life, to set them free from
    the power of demonic spirits, and to redeem them
    from sin and karma. By the miracle of dying in
    their place, Christ bore the penalty of their sin
    and shame. The perfect sinless Jesus restores
    God's power in the lives of humans and gives
    them a new quality of life connected spiritually
    to God Himself (John 1:14, 18, 29).

5. Humankind can have this power through
    repentance and faith in Christ as Lord and the
    source of constant provision. God, through His
    grace, gives this power freely, apart from human
    work or merit. God provides this power to humans
    through His Holy Spirit whom His disciples are
    to obey (John 1:10-13; 15:26; 16:12-15).

6. Believers are to share this gospel of power and
    freedom from karma with their relatives, friends,
    neighbours and nation (Acts 1:8; Ezek. 3:19-20).

Obviously a foundational teaching on the existence of God is vital. And the power encounter approach still requires time for diffusion, teaching and saturation.

The Bible abounds with illustrations of power encounter. For example, Gideon's destroying the family spirit grove; Elijah challenging the priests of Baal at Mount Carmel; Daniel's three bold friends in the fiery furnace; and Daniel proving the power of God in the lions' den. Truly above everything else, the mighty power of Christ in our lives is the crucial dynamic that will help Buddhists recognise the living Creator God.

Always remember though that patience is critical when working with Buddhist peoples. A time for diffusion of the message is usually necessary. Allowing time for gospel saturation over a period of time helps break down barriers of ignorance. Remember, few people brought up in a Buddhist culture will know much about the gospel, let alone anything true about it. We cannot expect people to make an immediate decision for Christ, across such a great barrier of understanding. In this respect personal interactions are essential. No amount of impersonal talking from afar by television or radio will understand and meet the needs and hopes of individuals and their families or communities.

Nine

Buddhist-Background Believers

Feeling at Home in Churches

It is important for churches to be open to receive Buddhist visitors or new believers from Buddhist backgrounds, whether Asian or Caucasian. Welcoming them with friendliness, showing sensitivity and providing genuine care to help them feel at home is essential.

Some Cautions

Christians offering help or support to Buddhists settling in the West must be careful not to be too controlling, overbearing or condescending. Overly aggressive and outgoing Westerners may overwhelm them. While coming alongside Buddhists with encouragement and assistance is commendable, always avoid having paternalistic attitudes toward them. Inviting them into homes for meals and taking them out will be appreciated. Where half a dozen or more Buddhist-background believers are involved, consider starting their own home fellowship or house church. Develop churches that help Buddhists feel comfortable in a Christian context. This may be more important for Asian immigrants than for Caucasian Buddhists already immersed in Western culture.

Keys to Follow-up

Where Buddhist seekers are receptive to the gospel, give them time to understand and choose Christ. It is unwise to pressure them to believe or be baptized prematurely. In following up their interest or commitments, be keen observers of what is going on in their lives, how they are acting or behaving, and what they are thinking about or struggling over. Learn from them about their cultural struggles and conflicts with their new faith. Ask questions and clarify their concerns. The best way to accomplish this is to listen attentively to them, discerning their heartfelt burdens.

Encourage them to talk about their problems. Get feedback on how they are growing in the faith and what kinds of opposition they are getting from their relatives and friends. Love them sincerely and support, encourage and nurture them in their development in the Christian walk. Above all, live a godly example before them with honesty and integrity. Pray for and with them. Exercise faith jointly and read and explain Scriptures together; mutual sharing is a great enhancer of relationships. Remember to show interest in and include their families and extended families in the prayers and discussions.

Returnees

Exchange students, university students and overseas graduate scholars studying in the West, will be returning to their home cultures at some point, as may Asian refugees going back to their homelands, either to visit their relatives or to work there. Where these have made commitments to Christ during their time in the West, Christians need to help prepare them for the return home and the situation they will face there as a believer.

Reverse Culture Shock

Not only have they themselves changed through influences in the intervening years of living in the West, but the cultures and situations in their families and homelands have also changed. As a result, returnees are likely to experience reverse culture shock. Re-entering their old culture produces some confusion and even disorientation and uneasiness over the changes that have occurred. The familiar is similar but not the same. New and different dimensions are now present in the home culture which also adds to this reverse culture shock. Given time and understanding this potential confusion will be resolved.

Reactive Families

Second, when they return to their homelands, new Christians may face some misunderstanding, opposition and even persecution from their Buddhist relatives. It is crucial for them to maintain a respectful, quiet and loving demeanour when they face any criticism or conflict. In Asia it is normal for parental control to be exercised over even adult children. Giving honour and respect to their parents and elders will be important in winning favour for their new-found faith.

Proactive Preparation

Planning in advance to integrate new believers and interested seekers into the Christian community in their home country will help considerably.

Two ways to be proactive are to build relationships and communicate early with the overseas families of returnees, and to build networks for incorporating them into churches or nurture groups ahead of time. The Japanese Christian Fellowship Network links returnees with a network of three former believing returnees already in the country. These three will already have experienced reverse culture shock and the pressures that come to Christian returnees. This helps in the process of reorientation. The triad of contacts also assists in integrating returnees into the friendly fellowships of groups or churches they attend. See the Resources section of further information on other agencies that may be able to help you.

Linking Fellowships

Where possible try to connect believing returnees with indigenous fellowships that are already culturally adapted to cater efficiently for Buddhist-background believers. Often local house churches or small groups in the returnees' homelands might be better than the closest church, especially if those are heavily Westernized ones.

Keeping Connections

Maintain correspondence with the returnees, at least every six months. Reaffirming friendship, expressing deep concern for their adjustments and continuing spiritual nurture can encourage them. Contact with their relatives is also important, particularly in Asia where the family is of greater importance than in the West. The earlier contact with families can be made, the better. From the start this helps allay the parents' fears about their offspring and it shows them how Christians are concerned to help and look after foreigners. It can also help reduce assumptions or fears Buddhist families may have about Christianity. This is a first step in relating to and reaching the Buddhist parents. The best evangelism is always done in the context of the family, even though in these cases it must, of necessity, be done long distance.

Remember the Family

Too many Christian workers fail to take the returnee's family and their concerns into account, working only with the individual student in the West. If good contact is maintained with the parents during the education process in the West, these Buddhists will be more approachable and sympathetic when their offspring show interest in church affairs or in seeking the Christian way, as well as when they return with their new-found faith. Communication with parents before the individuals return home is likely to find them much more amenable than if no prior connections have been built. This is an important, and often neglected, aspect of nurturing Buddhist-background believers.

Of course, always include the individual in your communication with their parents and ask their permission before making contact.

Encourage Meeting

Another idea is to encourage returnees from specific regions to meet together for fellowship and training every quarter or half year. Sharing their struggles and victories over problems encourages all returnees facing similar challenges. Networks can also be reaffirmed and developed during that period. Occasional personal contacts from the West can supplant these networks, but be careful not to substitute local networks. The more culturally sensitive the nurture is, the speedier will be the adjustments and growth in spiritual things.

Ten

PRAYING FOR BUDDHISTS

Buddhism is alive and well in the twenty-first century. At the same time Christianity in the West seems to be lacking in fervour and commitment. Probably the best exercise for Christians to practise in modern times is to commit to concerted prayer for our world and its needs today. Consecrated intercession for the Buddhist world and other neglected peoples demands much discipline and determination. Dedication to meditating on God's Word and translating that into supplication to the Lord is vital.

The Burden

An American professional couple, who are my encouraging friends, have for years prayed for missionaries and motivated their church to get involved in spreading the gospel. Normally they go to Europe for a vacation in mid-year. One summer they decided to change that routine pattern and go to Thailand instead. This literally transformed them. They reported that 'it was an eye-opening experience.' They loved the Thai people, but were shocked by the prevailing Buddhism and its enormous power over the populace. They saw temples galore, idols without number, abundant devotees, and no lack of saffron-robed priests. On their return they wrote,

'Our burden for the lost caught into Buddhism has grown exponentially. We have been intensely praying for the Buddhist world.'

Now that's a burden! Praying can often seem unconnected and distant, so why not go on a vision trip or get hold of some good resources to encourage yourself and others (see the Resources section for more information).

Tough Work

In lands where Buddhism prevails, the gospel languishes in its impact. Preaching the gospel there is like hitting a huge granite rock with a small green reed – the results are negligible. Generally today the church among Buddhist nations such as Japan, Thailand, Myanmar, Mongolia and other Buddhist peoples elsewhere is quite tiny, usually less than one per cent.

Animist tribal groups in Buddhist lands have been much more receptive to the gospel than the Buddhist people themselves. In Myanmar and Thailand, 97 per cent of the Christians there are tribal, though these ethnic peoples are in the minority. Recalculating Christian percentages from among Buddhist peoples without the Christianized tribes reveals a desperate need and a shockingly low proportion of Christians from among the Buddhist groups. But in recent years some encouraging signs of church growth have been occurring in pockets around the world. God is at work.

A burden to pray for these peoples is not only a significant, but also a strategic challenge. Tears of intercession with a deep love and concern for folk Buddhists worldwide will move the church forward on its knees. Andrew Murray said, 'He who prays most helps most.' Will you join in praying for the Buddhist world?

Praying Biblically

1. Pray for leaders, governments and kings of Buddhist lands to rule righteously, fairly and honestly, so that their people may live in peace, with dignity, and in right relationships with each other and God. Consider 1 Timothy 2:1-8; Genesis 12:2-3; Jeremiah 4:2.

2. Praise God that 'a people for his name' will be called from every Buddhist nation, tribe, people and tongue. See Revelation 7:9-10.

3. Immobilise the forces of darkness through prayer, resisting all demonic rulers and spiritual powers which influence our world, including Buddhists. Wait on Christ in accordance with Ephesians 6:12-13; Daniel 10:13, 20.

4. Call on God to melt down spiritual defences and human philosophies which argue against God, and which produce barriers of resistance through social solidarity. See 2 Corinthians 10:4-5.

5. Claim Christ's complete victory over all demonic powers that blind and enslave billions of people worldwide. See Colossians 2:15.

6. Pray out 'God-sent, willing, skilful workers' for each of many hundreds of neglected Buddhist people groups across the globe. See Matthew 9:38.

7. Intercede for lasting fruit from the labour and sacrifice of Christ's workers from many agencies and servants of the church from all nations working among Buddhist groups. See John 12:24.

8. Plead with God to open eyes to see the true and living Creator and Christ, the unique Saviour. See Ephesians 1:17-23.

9. Believe God to enlighten the minds of Buddhists about the folly of making images, bowing down to them, and worshipping the forces behind them. See Psalms 115:4-8.

10. Ask God to help Christians discern the biblical differences between Buddhist terms and the meaning of Christ's gospel, so they can intelligently communicate the Good News. See Proverbs 2:2-3; 2 Timothy 2:7.

11. Pray for Buddhist hearts and minds to understand the gospel, especially the doctrines of Christ's incarnation, sacrificial substitution, and the redemption He bought for all people. See Galatians 3:13; 1 Peter 1:18-25, 2:24.

12. Intercede for Buddhists and their families to come to faith in Christ, repenting from their total dependence on their own good works. Pray for the healing of their deep hurts, suffering and felt needs. See Ephesians 2:8-9.

13. Pray for the preserving, protection and nurture of new believers from Buddhist cultures, claiming

God's protective 'wall of fire around them'. See Zechariah 2:5; Psalms 91.

14. Ask that believers will share the gospel as bold witnesses to their Buddhist families, friends and neighbours. See Acts 4:29-31.

15. Uphold all Christians in Buddhist lands before the throne of God that they will exhibit holy, disciplined lifestyles as examples and models of Christ. See 2 Corinthians 3:2-3; 1 Peter 1:15-16; 2:21.

16. Plead with God to multiply churches and begin church-planting movements among each Buddhist people group. See Matthew 16:18; 1 Peter 2:9-10.

17. Intercede for the raising up of house fellowships and national church leaders, many of them unpaid, to train and care for God's flocks and to extend the church into each Buddhist group. See Acts 20:27-32; 1 Peter 5:1-4.

Conclusion

How can we apply this to daily life? Three basic applications call believers to pray, adapt and witness.

First the spiritual conflict demands concentrated prayer to break the controlling spirit forces of darkness in the heavenlies. God has answered and will answer prayer, but the demonic forces may strongly hinder and temporarily frustrate His answers from being appropriated at times (Dan. 9:3-4; 17-23). Pray God will break down these powers and free hearts to hear the Word of God through the Holy Spirit.

Second is the socio-cultural clash. This solid social coherence comes largely from the religious thinking. To be Burmese means to be Buddhist. To change religious allegiance is like becoming a traitor to one's own nation. Will natural disasters and human crises be the instruments that prepare hearts to seek Creator God? There are signs of such changes at work today.

Third is the bold, though humble, witness of the gospel through loving works and words. A dynamic experience with the living Lord can change people. Let those prophetic advocates arise, like Elijah, to demonstrate power encounters. Many lessons are to be learned. More will be gained through sympathetic appreciation of the people than by cold logic. A cultural sensitivity should be welded to incarnational witness based on a deep biblical foundation.

This requires a person-centred approach while maintaining a truth-centred gospel. To find the best evangelistic methods for each Buddhist population, much research and careful experimentation should be implemented speedily. All this calls today's teachers, preachers and witnesses in Asia to a new practical task of dealing with various issues in communication so that significant pockets of population can and will seek Jesus Christ and become functional members of His church.

Resources

Books

A Pocket Guide to World Religions, Winifred Corduan, IVP, 2006

Communicating Christ in the Buddhist World, Paul De Neui and David Lim, William Carey Library, 2006

Communicating Christ Through Story and Song, Paul H. DeNeui, ed, William Carey Library, 2008

Compact Guide to World Religions, Dean Halverson, Bethany House, 1996

From Buddha to Jesus: An insider's view of Buddhism and Christianity, Steve Cioccolanti, Boosurge Llc, 2008

Jesus in a New Age, Dalai Lama World: Defending and Sharing Christ with Buddhists M. Tsering, Interserve, 2006. Previously published as *Sharing Christ in the Tibetan Buddhist World*.

Poles Apart, John Davis, Theological Book Trust, 1998

Sharing Jesus Effectively in the Buddhist World, David Lim, Steve Spaulding, & Paul De Neui, eds., William Carey Library, 2005

Sharing Jesus Holistically with the Buddhist World, David Lim and Steve Spaulding, William Carey Library, 2005

Sharing Jesus in the Buddhist World, David Lim and Steve Spaulding, eds., William Carey Library, 2003

Siamese Gold: The Church in Thailand, Alex G. Smith, Kanok Bannasan Publishing, 2004

The Cross and the Lotus, Ravi Zacharias, Multnomah Publishers, 2001

The Spirit of Buddhism: A Christian Perspective on Buddhist Thought, David Burnett, Monarch, revised 2007

Prayer Resources

Some resources for stimulating information and materials of Christian concern for Buddhists include:

Tearing Down Strongholds: Prayer for Buddhists, Elizabeth Wagner, Living Books for All. Available from PO Box 98425 (TST) Kowloon, Hong Kong.

A Billion Wait: A Prayer Guide for the Buddhist World, SEANET, 2002. To order email: mgfd@gmx.net

Peoples of the Buddhist World, Paul Hattaway, Piquant, 2004

Vision Trips

If you would like to spend a week or more experiencing Buddhist cultures first-hand, the contact omf@omf.org.uk or visit www.omf.org for more information. OMF can co-ordinate a variety of experiences from visiting Buddhist countries to working amongst Buddhists in the UK.

Websites and Online Resources

The Lausanne Movement
Christian Witness to Buddhists, Lausanne Occasional Paper 15, http://www.lausanne.org/pattaya-1980/lop-15.html.
For other documents see http://www.lausanne.org/documents.html

Buddha Book
http://www.buddhabook.org/
Explains the gospel to Buddhists, connects Buddhist-background believers and provides discussion forums.

One Billion Wait
www.onebillionwait.org
A website giving information, facts, figures, stories and resources to help Christians understand, pray for and communicate effectively with Buddhists.

Sonrise Centre for Buddhist Studies
http://www.sonrisecenter.org/aboutus-overview.html
An organisation whose vision is to see a church established and leadership discipled among every unreached Buddhist people group. Their website

contains information to equip the Christian community for ministry amongst Buddhists, enabling them to intelligently share the gospel.

Foreign Language Bibles and Study Materials

Bamboo Resource Centre
591 Dominion Road
Balmoral
Auckland
New Zealand
09 630 5997
nz-bamboo@omf.net
www.bamboo.co.nz

Scripture Gift Mission
www.sgm.org

Contacts

Australia:
OMF
PO Box 849, Epping, NSW 1710
Tel: 02 9868 4777
Email: au@omf.net
www.au.omf.org

Canada:
OMF International
5155 Spectrum Way
Building 21
Mississauga
ONT L4W 5A1
Toll free: 1 888 657 8010
Email: omfcanada@omf.ca
www.ca.omf.org

Miss Fee Reeds
277 St George St.
Apt 804
Toronto ON.
M5R 2R1
Tel. (+001) 416 972 9561
Fee works with international students as part of IVCF.

Hong Kong:
OMF International
PO Box 70505
Kowloon Central PO
Hong Kong
Tel: 852 2398 1823
Email: hk@omf.net
www.omf.org.hk

Malaysia:
OMF International
3A Jalan Nipah, off Jalan Ampang,
55000, Kuala Lumpur
Tel: 603 4257 4263
Email: my@omf.net
www.omf.org.my

New Zealand:
OMF International
PO Box 10159,
Dominion Road,
Balmoral,
Auckland, 1030
Tel: 09 630 5778
Email: omfnz@omf.net
www.nz.omf.org
www.noordinarylife.org

Philippines:
OMF International
QCCPO Box 1997-1159,
1100 Quezon City, M.M.
Tel: 632 951 0782
Email: ph-hc@omf.net
www.omf.org.ph

Singapore:
OMF International
2 Cluny Road,
Singapore 259570
Tel: 65 6475 4592
Email: sno@omf.net
www.sg.omf.org

UK:
OMF International
Station Approach
Borough Green,
Kent
TN15 8BG
Tel: 01732 887299
Email: omf@omf.org.uk
www.omf.org.uk

OMF's Diaspora Ministries Team in the UK runs Church Training Days to enable British Christians to more effectively reach out to Chinese and other East Asians. For details of the current schedule or information on organising a training day in your area, please contact the Diaspora Ministries Team as above.

The team can also give help, advice and speak at meetings.

UCCF Professional Groups
38 De Montfort Street
Leicester
LE1 7GP
UK
Tel: 0116 2551700
Fax: 0116 2255672
Email: email@uccf.org.uk
www.uccf.org.uk/graduates/professionalgroups.php

Friends International
3 Crescent Stables
139 Upper Richmond Road
Putney
London SW15 2TN
UK
Tel: 0181 7803511
Email: info@friendsinternational.org.uk
www.friendsinternational.org.uk

Friends International work with international students living in the UK. They can suggest events for your friend to go to, and may know of other Japanese students living nearby, including others who are Christians or seekers.

IFES: UK
38 De Montfort Street
Leicester
LE1 7GP
UK
Phone: +44 116 255 1700
Email: email@uccf.org.uk
www.uccf.org.uk

IFES is a fellowship of students, staff and supporters that aims
to bring glory to God by establishing a vibrant gospel witness
among students in every nation.

USA:
OMF International
10 West Dry Creek Circle,
Littleton,
CO 80120-4413
Toll free: 1 800 422 5330
Email: buddhism@omf.org
www.omf.org/us

International Students, Inc.
PO Box C
Colorado Springs
CO 80901
Phone: 719 576 2700
Fax: 719 576 5363

Glossary

Anatta	The concept of no-self. The belief that there is no lasting soul, spirit, or individual nature that defines an individual human or survives beyond death.
Anicca	The concept of impermanence. The belief that everything is in a constant state of flux, and nothing exists independently.
Arupa	A type of Brahma that is formless.
Asalha	Asalha Puja Day, also known as Dharma Day, celebrates the first teaching of the Buddha and is one of the most important festivals in Theravada Buddhism.
Asura	A type of power-seeking demon. Opposite to a deva.
Avalokiteshvara	The bodhisattva of compassion. One of the most highly revered bodhisattvas in Mahayana Buddhism. Also known as Kwan Yin, Kuan Yin or Guan Yin (China), Chenrezig (Tibet), Kannon or Kanzeon (Japan) and Avolokiteshvara.
Avolokiteshvara	See Avalokiteshvara
Avijja	The concept of ignorance. The lack of *Vidya* or acquired skills, learning, wisdom and knowledge.
Bhavana	See meditation.
Bhumi	The planes of existence into which individuals are reborn. There are considered to be thirty-one separate *Bhumis*.

Bodhi	Perfect wisdom or insight, the state of enlightenment, by which a person becomes a Buddha, and finally ends the cycle of death and rebirth, and enters nirvana.
Bodhisattva	An enlightened being. In Mahayana Buddhism, they may delay their going to nirvana in order to help others who cannot get there by their own merit.
Brahma	Deities occupying the non-sensuous heaven realms. Also, a supreme and eternal essence or spirit of the universe, chief god of Hindu trinity, Hindu creator of the universe.
Brahmans	Members of the priestly highest Hindu caste.
Buddha	Meaning awakened one who has achieved *bodhi*. The name given to Siddhartha Gautama, the historically recorded Buddha, who reached enlightenment, and first taught the Four Noble Truths. In Mahayana, the name given to anyone who achieves enlightenment.
Ch'an	See Zen.
Chakra	Also known as the Wheel of Dharma or the Wheel of Law. The wheel has a central hub symbolising discipline, eight spokes, representing the Eightfold Path and an outer rim, symbolic of the mindfulness that holds everything together. The Chakra is one of the eight auspicious symbols in Tibetan Buddhism.
Dalai Lama	Literally 'Ocean' or 'great teacher,' honorary title of the head of Geluk lineage in Tibetan Buddhism, believed to be the current incarnation of a long line of Tulkus, or Buddhist Masters. These masters have become exempt from the cycle of Samsara, but have chosen to be reborn in order to enlighten others. He is also the official leader of the Tibetan government-in-exile, or the Central Tibetan Administration (CTA).
Deva	A type of godlike being or demi-god that is more powerful and more content than a human.
Dharma	The teachings of the Buddha that lead to enlightenment. Also written as Dhamma.

Dukkha	The concept of suffering. The nature of existence according to the first of the Four Noble Truths.
Eightfold Path	The teachings of Buddha said to lead to enlightenment and cessation of suffering.
Enlightenment	Described as awakening, or realisation of the true nature of the universe. It releases the individual from the Cycle of Samsara.
Four Noble Truths	The fundamental teachings of Buddhism which Buddha received at enlightenment.
Gautama Siddhartha	A Hindu prince, he was enlightened and became the historically recorded Buddha. Also spelt Gotama Siddhatta.
Great Renunciation	When Gautama Siddhartha left the palace and his abundant life to live as an ascetic.
Hananim	The Korean name for God used during a period of Christian outreach to Korean Buddhists in the early twentieth century.
Heaven	In Buddhism there are several heavens. A person is reborn into these as a result of their good karma. The person will remain in the heaven until the karma is 'used up'. They will then be reborn into a lower level of existence as a result of bad karma working itself out. You cannot reach enlightenment from any of these heavens.
Hell	In Buddhism there are many hells or Narakas. A person is reborn into these as a result of their bad karma. The person will remain in the hell until the karma is 'used up'. They will then be reborn into a higher level of existence as a result of good karma working itself out.
Jhanic bliss	As a result of living a contemplative lifestyle, Buddha said that four jhanic states could be achieved. In these states the body is filled with rapture, pleasure, calm and awareness.
Kama-Loka	Are realms of sensual gratification and pleasure inhabited by devas.

Karma	A law of cause and effect. It determines a person's future based on their past actions, thoughts and motives. Karma cannot be undone, altered, avoided or forgiven. Good karma does not cancel out bad karma – both will work their consequences through. Also spelt *Kamma*.
Kathina	A festival in Theravada Buddhism. It falls in October, at the end of *Vassa*, the rainy season. People will show gratitude to the monks by bringing alms to the temple.
Kattika	A festival in Theravada Buddhism. It commemorates the first Buddhist missionaries who set out to spread the Buddha's teachings.
Kulpa	A Buddhist era: a vast period of time measuring time between earthly appearances of a Buddha or a larger-scale whole world cycle. Also spelt kalpa.
Kwan Yin	See Avalokiteshvara
Lama	Meaning 'teacher', it is the name given to people teaching the Dharma in Tibetan forms.
Loka	A realm or plane of existence.
Mahayana	Also known as Northern or Eastern Buddhism. It is a more liberal school of Buddhism and includes Tendai, Zen, Pure Land, Nichiren, Soka Gakkai and Tibetan Buddhism, as well as most of the branches of folk Buddhism.
Mandala	Elaborate and geometric circular designs symbolising the universe. They are often made in sand and used as meditation aids.
Mani Stones	Used in Tibetan Buddhism, they are stones inscribed with prayers or mantras. They are often placed along roads, hills or rivers, or heaped together as an offering to the spirits.
Mantra	A powerful syllable, word, phrase or poem that will be repeated or chanted, to remove distracting thoughts and clear the mind.
Manussa-Loka	The human realm of existence.

Meditation	One of the basic practices of Buddhism. Concentration and the use of *mantras* and postures aims to achieve tranquillity and insight. Referred to as *bhavana*.
Mucilinda	Mucilinda was a naga who protected the Buddha from the elements after his enlightenment. Four weeks after Buddha began meditating under the Bodhi tree, the heavens darkened for seven days, and a storm arose. *Mucilinda*, the king of serpents, came from beneath the earth and protected the Buddha. When the storm cleared, the serpent assumed his human form, bowed before the Buddha, and returned beneath the earth.
Mudras	Postures used during meditation. They are signs having symbolic meaning.
Naga	A cobra-like serpent, often depicted with multiple heads. The naga are powerful and capable of adopting human form. See Mucilinda.
Naraka	Sanskrit for the underworlds or hells. Known as *Niraya* in the Pali language.
Niraya	See *Naraka*
Nirvana	Literally 'extinguished'. The goal of Buddhism. A state of perfect inner stillness and peace when enlightenment is reached and all craving and desire ceases. True reality is known and the individual is released from the Cycle of Samsara . Also known as *Nipaan*.
Pali Canon	The standard collection of scriptures in Theravada Buddhism, preserved in the Pali language.
Phrachao	A Thai term referring to 'something which one fears and must beseech or flatter, an instinct among all thinking beings'/God.
Prayer Wheel	A hollow metal cylinder mounted on a rod handle containing a mantra printed on a tightly wound scroll. Spinning a prayer wheel is considered the same as reciting the mantra aloud. Used primarily in Tibetan Buddhism, carried during devotional activities.

Rupa	Devas with form.
Samatha	Meaning 'calm abiding'. A state of concentration. Also spelt shamatha.
Samsara	The cycle of birth, death and rebirth. It generates suffering and can only be escaped by attaining enlightenment.
Sangha	Meaning 'assembly'. It is used to refer to the Buddhist community, or a group of practitioners within a certain monastery or school.
Sila	The basic moral behaviours used to train individuals to lead a more devoted lifestyle.
Skandhas	The five aggregates that make up human existence: matter (form), sensations (feelings), perception, mental formation (impulses) and consciousness. Also known as *khandas*.
Stupa	A dome-shaped monument commemorating the death of Buddha.
Sunyatta	The Mahayana doctrine of emptiness. The concept of being boundless or open. Stemming from the concept of *anatta*, or no-self.
Sutra	Buddhist scriptures, consisting of discourses between Buddha and his followers.
Swastika	A common auspicious Buddhist symbol with many meanings: *Dharma*, universal harmony, peace, prosperity, love, resignation, balance of opposites, longevity and eternity.
Tangka	Painted scrolls used for meditation, worship and purification of the soul. They often depict deities and are mostly used in Tibetan Buddhism.
Tantras	Magically based spiritual practices and ritual acts aimed at removing ignorance and achieving enlightenment.

The Middle Way	The practice of non-extremism.
The Way	Also known as Tao or Dao. A philosophical and religious tradition, referring to the universal principle, truth or nature of things; closely allied to Zen or Ch'an
Theravada	Also known as Southern Buddhism, it is the more conservative school of Buddhism.
Tibetan Buddhism	Also known as Lamaism, Tantrism, Vajrayana, or Mantrayana. Led by the Lamas.
Titans	See asura.
Tripitaka	Meaning Three Baskets. A term used in the West to refer to the Buddhist canon of scripture.
Vesakha	A festival celebrating the Buddha's birth, enlightenment, and passing into nirvana. It falls in April/May.
Vinaya	Meaning 'discipline', it is the Buddha's teaching which is used as behavioural rules for the sangha.
Vinyaan	Intelligence, knowledge, consciousness, thought, mind, spirit (In Thai, *winyaan* means 'soul')
Vipassana	Insight into the true nature of reality.
Yantras	Instruments and symbols used to focus the mind during meditation.
Zen	A form of Mahayana Buddhism that emphasizes experiential knowledge, achieved through meditation, rather than theoretical knowledge, as the route to enlightenment. Zen is the Japanese name, while it is referred to as Ch'an in China.

A Christian's Pocket Guide to

the Chinese

OMF

A Christian's Pocket Guide to the Chinese

OMF

If you go to the Wangfujing shopping centre in Beijing then you will find it bustling with shoppers and lined with expensive stores. Taking a break from the throng you can stop for a coffee at Starbucks or have a snack at McDonald's. These are all signs of an increasing 'Westernisation' in China but behind the scenes there is also a spiritual transformation taking place.

This book is designed to help you if you have regular interaction with people from China. Firstly, it gives you a brief outline of the major changes that have taken place in recent history so that you can understand their cultural background.

Secondly, it looks at Chinese students in more detail. Why are they in your schools and universities? Where in China do they come from and what difference does that make? What has changed in their attitude to study? What is their lifestyle likely to be like? What will they think of you?

Thirdly, it looks at how best to befriend Chinese people and make them welcome in your country and fourthly, how best to engage them in discussion (including a valuable FAQ section with answers and further resources to go to), and fifthly, how to speak on spiritual topics.

ISBN 978-1-84550-315-4

A Christian's
Pocket Guide to

the Japanese

OMF

A Christian's Pocket Guide to the Japanese

OMF

Globalisation means that increasingly we meet people from a wider variety of nations and cultures.

The manufacturing revolution that has seen Japan become one of the top industrialised nations in the world means that more Japanese people are travelling abroad and more people are travelling to Japan.

What should Christians know about the Japanese? That question is answered by this book.

A Christian's Pocket Guide to the Japanese firstly looks at the history, culture and religions common in Japan – and their attitude to Christianity.

Secondly, it gives guidance on how to befriend Japanese people (including a life-saving 'Dos' and 'Don'ts' section) and thirdly how best to talk to them about Christianity itself.

There are also useful appendices with suggested further reading and how to lead a Bible study.

If you meet people from Japan at work, school or socially – or if you travel to Japan – then this is an invaluable book.

ISBN 978-1-84550-316-1

A Christian's
Pocket Guide to

Islam

Patrick Sookhdeo

A Christian's Pocket Guide to Islam

PATRICK SOOKHDEO

Have you ever watched a TV programme or read a newspaper article where a commentator clumsily illustrates his complete ignorance of Christianity and its claims?

How often have you rolled your eyes and immediately discounted what is being said, saying to yourself 'Well, why should I listen to them when they obviously haven't got a clue!' How, then, can we expect to witness effectively to those of the Muslim faith if all that we know of Islam is picked up from passing references in the media?

This fascinating book provides Christians with a simple description of the origins of Islam, what Muslims believe and how it affects their attitudes, worldview, everyday life and culture. Practical guidelines are given for relating to Muslims in a culturally appropriate way, as well as for witnessing effectively and caring for converts.

Patrick Sookhdeo is Director of the Institute for the Study of Islam and Christianity, a Christian research institute specialising in the status of Christian minorities in the Muslim world. Dr Sookhdeo is a well-known lecturer and author who holds a Ph.D. from London University's School of Oriental and African Studies and a D.D. from Western Seminary, Oregon, USA.

ISBN 978-1-84550-119-8

OMF

OMF International works in most East Asian countries, and among East Asian peoples around the world. It was founded by James Hudson Taylor in 1865 as the China Inland Mission. Our purpose is to glorify God through the urgent evangelisation of East Asia's billions.

In line with this, OMF Publishing seeks to motivate and equip Christians to make disciples of all peoples. Publications include:

- stories and biographies showing God at work in East Asia
- the biblical basis of mission and mission issues
- the growth and development of the church in Asia
- studies of Asian culture and religion

Books, booklets, articles and free downloads can be found on our website at www.omf.org

Christian Focus Publications

publishes books for all ages

Our mission statement –

STAYING FAITHFUL

In dependence upon God we seek to impact the world through literature faithful to His infallible Word, the Bible. Our aim is to ensure that the LORD Jesus Christ is presented as the only hope to obtain forgiveness of sin, live a useful life and look forward to heaven with Him.

REACHING OUT

Christ's last command requires us to reach out to our world with His gospel. We seek to help fulfil that by publishing books that point people towards Jesus and help them develop a Christ-like maturity. We aim to equip all levels of readers for life, work, ministry and mission.

Books in our adult range are published in three imprints.

Christian Focus contains popular works including biographies, commentaries, basic doctrine and Christian living. Our children's books are also published in this imprint.

Mentor focuses on books written at a level suitable for Bible College and seminary students, pastors, and other serious readers. The imprint includes commentaries, doctrinal studies, examination of current issues and church history.

Christian Heritage contains classic writings from the past.

Christian Focus Publications Ltd,
Geanies House, Fearn, Ross-shire,
IV20 1TW, Scotland, United Kingdom
info@christianfocus.com
www.christianfocus.com